The Observer's Pocket Series

AIRCRAFT

OBSERVER'S BOOKS

NATURAL HISTORY
Birds · Birds' Eggs · Wild Animals · Zoo Animals
Farm Animals · Freshwater Fishes · Sea Fishes
Tropical Fishes · Butterflies · Larger Moths · Caterpillars
Insects · Pond Life · Sea and Seashore · Seashells · Pets
Dogs · Horses and Ponies · Cats · Trees · Wild Flowers
Grasses · Mushrooms · Lichens · Cacti · Garden Flowers
Flowering Shrubs · Vegetables · Herbs · House Plants
Geology · Rocks and Minerals · Fossils · Weather
Astronomy · Roses

SPORT
Soccer · Cricket · Golf · Coarse Fishing · Fly Fishing
Sea Fishing · Show Jumping · Motor Sport

TRANSPORT
Automobiles · Aircraft · Commercial Vehicles
Motorcycles · Steam Locomotives · Ships · Small Craft
Manned Spaceflight · Unmanned Spaceflight

ARCHITECTURE
Architecture · Churches · Cathedrals · Castles

COLLECTING
Awards and Medals · Coins · Firearms · Furniture
Postage Stamps · Glass · Pottery and Porcelain

ARTS AND CRAFTS
Music · Painting · Modern Art · Sewing · Jazz · Big Bands

HISTORY AND GENERAL INTEREST
Ancient Britain · Flags · Heraldry · European Costume

TRAVEL
London · Tourist Atlas GB · Lake District · Cotswolds
Devon and Cornwall

The Observer's Book of

AIRCRAFT

COMPILED BY
WILLIAM GREEN

WITH SILHOUETTES BY
DENNIS PUNNETT

DESCRIBING 140 AIRCRAFT
WITH 247 ILLUSTRATIONS

1980 EDITION

FREDERICK WARNE

© FREDERICK WARNE & CO LTD
LONDON, ENGLAND
1980

Twenty-ninth edition 1980

LIBRARY OF CONGRESS CATALOG CARD NO: 57 4425

ISBN 0 7232 1604 5

Printed in Great Britain

INTRODUCTION TO THE 1980 EDITION

As this, the twenty-ninth annual edition of *The Observer's Book of Aircraft*, appears, we have entered a new decade, and when it is considered that the past four-score years have embraced the entire history of powered heavier-than-air flight, few would deny that decades are *long* periods of time in terms of aviation development. Aeronautical progress would seem to lose none of its dynamism with their passage, but increasing aircraft sophistication is inevitably being accompanied by lengthening time spans for translation from drawing board to service use—to bring a major new commercial transport or high-performance military aircraft to fruition nowadays demands all of a decade and more.

The reduction in the number of *entirely* new aircraft types as a result of this more protractive development process is inevitable and has become progressively more noticeable as the 'seventies drew to a close. Conversely, variations on established themes multiplied with the commensurate lengthening of aircraft production lives. Furthermore, aircraft are now being upgraded in capability and reinstated in production after lapses of many years (eg, Transall, Atlantic and Jetstream), while the practice is increasing of extending the service lives of aircraft no longer in production by means of re-engining, structural stretching, the application of aerodynamic improvements, or a combination of all of these.

Such trends have been faithfully reflected by the content of the successive *Observer's Books* of the 'seventies, and will be particularly apparent in perusing the pages of this, the first edition of the 'eighties. Those aircraft types to be found on the following pages that are *totally* new to the *Observer's Book* may be counted on the fingers of the hands, but the proportion of new versions of *established* aircraft is higher than in any preceding edition.

In the first edition of a new decade, it is tempting to speculate on the changes in the aviation scene that are likely to take place over the coming 10 years, and little crystal-gazing is called for to conjecture that the present trend towards fewer completely new types in favour of progressive development of proven models will continue through the 'eighties. Little else may be predicted with any degree of certainty, however, for the 'seventies demonstrated that the evolution of aviation over a half-score years may be influenced less by technological advances than by unforeseen world events, not least of which having been the recurrent fuel crises and worldwide inflation.

Unpropitious portents for the well-being of aviation though such may have seemed, as this new decade sees birth, mass air travel continues to grow apace and the world market for aircraft in every category, from the largest airliners through business executive transports to helicopters and light aircraft, has never been more buoyant. Who is to say what new shapes will be seen in the skies of the 'eighties, but whatever these may be, it is hoped that they will be duly recorded in future editions of *The Observer's Book of Aircraft*.

WILLIAM GREEN

AERITALIA G.222

Country of Origin: Italy.

Type: General-purpose military transport.

Power Plant: (G.222L) Two 3,800 shp (flat-rated from 5,060 shp) Rolls-Royce Tyne RTy 20 (Mk. 801) turboprops.

Performance: (G.222L) Max. cruising speed (at 54,013 lb/24 500 kg), 350 mph (563 km/h) at 20,000 ft (6 095 m); range with max payload (15,430 lb/7 000 kg) and 10% reserves, 825 mls (1 327 km) at 20,000 ft (6 095 m), with 53 fully-equipped troops and 10% reserves, 1,060 mls (1 705 km); ferry range, 3,175 mls (5 110 km); initial climb at max take-off weight, 2,050 ft/min (10,4 m/sec).

Weights: Operational empty, 39,682 lb (18 000 kg); max. take-off, 61,730 lb (28 000 kg).

Accommodation: Flight crew of three–four and 53 fully-equipped troops, 42 paratroops or 36 casualty stretchers plus four medical attendants.

Status: Prototype G.222L (conversion of 34th production G.222 airframe) scheduled to fly second quarter of 1980, with deliveries against order for 20 from Libya to commence early 1981 at one per month. Seventy-four (all versions) laid down of which 34 built at Caselle and remainder being built at Pomigliano d'Arco, with some 35 delivered by beginning of 1980.

Notes: Variants of standard General Electric T64-P4D-powered G.222 (see 1978 edition) are the G.222VS electronic-countermeasures version (illustrated above) and G.222RM flight inspection aircraft. The G.222L is illustrated opposite.

AERITALIA G.222L

Dimensions: Span, 94 ft 2 in (28,70 m); length, 74 ft 5½ in (22,70 m); height, 32 ft 1¾ in (9,80 m); wing area, 882·64 sq ft (82,00 m²).

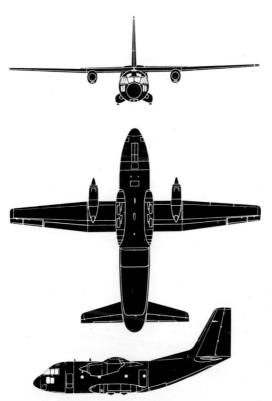

AERMACCHI MB 339

Country of Origin: Italy.

Type: Two-seat basic and advanced trainer.

Power Plant: One 4,000 lb (1 814 kg) Fiat-built Rolls-Royce Viper 632-43 turbojet.

Performance: Max. speed (clean configuration), 558 mph (898 km/h) at sea level, 508 mph (817 km/h) at 30,000 ft (9 145 m) or Mach 0·77; max. range (clean configuration), 1,094 mls (1 760 km), (ferry configuration with two 143 Imp gal/650 l pylon tanks), 1,310 mls (2 110 km); initial climb, 6,600 ft/min (33,5 m/sec); service ceiling, 47,500 ft (14 630 m).

Weights: Empty equipped, 6,883 lb (3 125 kg); loaded (clean), 9,700 lb (4 400 kg); max. take-off, 13,000 lb (5 897 kg).

Armament: For armament training and light strike roles a maximum of 4,000 lb (1 815 kg) may be distributed between six underwing stations, the inner and mid stations being of 750 lb (340 kg) capacity and the outer stations being of 500 lb (230 kg) capacity.

Status: Two prototypes flown on August 12, 1976, and May 20, 1977, respectively, and first of six pre-series aircraft flown on July 20, 1978, with first two examples accepted by Italian Air Force on August 9, 1979. Production scheduled to attain four monthly by end of 1980, with last of 100 for Italian Air Force being delivered late 1982.

Notes: Based on the airframe of the earlier MB 326 and incorporating the strengthened structure of the MB 326K, the MB 339 incorporates an entirely redesigned forward fuselage providing vertically staggered seats for pupil and instructor.

AERMACCHI MB 339

Dimensions: Span, 35 ft 7 in (10,86 m); length, 36 ft 0 in (10,97 m); height, 13 ft 1 in (3,99 m); wing area, 207·74 sq ft (19,30 m²).

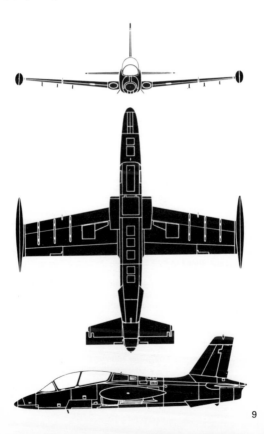

9

AÉROSPATIALE FOUGA 90

Country of Origin: France.
Type: Tandem two-seat basic trainer.
Power Plant: Two 1,742 lb (790 kg) Turboméca Astafan IVG turbofans.
Performance: Max. speed, 431 mph (694 km/h) at 20,000 ft (6 095 m), 408 mph (657 km/h) at sea level; initial climb, 4,250 ft/min (21,6 m/sec); range (at economic cruise), 1,305 mls (2 100 km); endurance (without reserves), 3 hrs.
Weights: Empty equipped, 5,842 lb (2 650 kg); normal loaded, 8,377 lb (3 800 kg); max. take-off, 9,259 lb (4 200 kg).
Armament: For armament training and light attack roles four wing hardpoints are provided, the inboard hardpoints being of 551 lb (250 kg) capacity and the outboard points being of 331 lb (150 kg) capacity, external ordnance being limited to 1,764 lb (800 kg). Provision for optional 30-mm DEFA 553 cannon with 150 rounds in starboard side of forward fuselage.
Status: Prototype flown on August 20, 1978, with pre-series aircraft scheduled to fly September 1980, and first production aircraft following from October 1981.
Notes: Developed as a private-venture, the Fouga 90 retains the configuration and much of the aerodynamic design of the CM 170 Magister, the prototype utilising the wing and under-carriage of the Super Magister. The production Fouga 90 (illustrated by the general arrangement silhouette opposite) has a structurally redesigned wing incorporating leading-edge fuel tanks replacing the wingtip tanks of the earlier trainer, a recontoured nose, a one-piece sideways-hinged canopy over both cockpits, a revised undercarriage and other changes. No production orders had been announced at the time of closing for press.

AÉROSPATIALE FOUGA 90

Dimensions: Span, 39 ft 6 in (12,04 m); length, 34 ft $3\frac{4}{8}$ in (10,46 m); height, 10 ft $1\frac{1}{4}$ in (3,08 m); wing area, 198·06 sq ft (18,40 m²).

AÉROSPATIALE (SOCATA) TB 10
TOBAGO

Country of Origin: France.
Type: Light cabin monoplane.
Power Plant: One 180 hp Avco Lycoming O–320–A1AD four-cylinder horizontally-opposed engine.
Performance: Max. speed, 153 mph (247 km/h); cruising speed (75% power), 146 mph (235 km/h), (65% power), 137 mph (220 km/h); initial climb, 790 ft/min (4,01 m/sec); service ceiling, 13,123 ft (4 000 m); max. range, 668 mls (1 075 km).
Weights: Empty, 1,477 lb (670 kg); max. take-off, 2,535 lb (1 150 kg).
Accommodation: Pilot and passenger in side-by-side individual seats with bench-type seating at rear of cabin for two/three passengers. Baggage compartment aft of cabin.
Status: The prototype TB 10 Tobago was flown on February 23, 1977, production deliveries commencing early 1979, approximately 50 having been delivered by beginning of 1980.
Notes: Manufactured by SOCATA, the general aviation division of Aérospatiale, the TB 10 Tobago is the first in a family of light cabin monoplanes, which, possessing structural commonality, will differ primarily in the type and power of engine installed. The first of these variants is the TB 9 Tampico with a 160 hp Lycoming O–320–D2A engine which was certificated late 1979. Production rate of the Tobago and Tampico combined was scheduled to attain 10 monthly by the beginning of 1980.

12

AÉROSPATIALE (SOCATA) TB 10 TOBAGO

Dimensions: Span, 32 ft 0¼ in (9,76 m); length, 25 ft 0¾ in (7,64 m); height, 9 ft 6¼ in (2,90 m); wing area, 128·1 sq ft (11,9 m²).

AÉROSPATIALE TB 30 EPSILON

Country of Origin: France.

Type: Tandem two-seat primary-basic trainer.

Power Plant: One 300 hp Avco Lycoming AEIO-540-L1A5-D six-cylinder horizontally-opposed engine.

Performance: (Estimated) Max. speed, 228 mph (367 km/h) at sea level; initial climb, 1,900 ft/min (9,65 m/sec); service ceiling, 20,100 ft (6 400 m); endurance (with reserves) at 75% power, 3·0 hrs at 5,000 ft (1 640 m); max. range, 808 mls (1 300 km).

Weights: Normal loaded, 2,540 lb (1 152 kg).

Status: The first of two prototypes of the TB 30 built by the SOCATA general aviation division of Aérospatiale was scheduled to commence its flight test programme at the end of 1979, current planning calling for the commencement of series production during the second half of 1980, with deliveries to the *Armée de l'Air* in 1981.

Notes: Designed to meet the requirements of the so-called *Epsilon* programme for a trainer to be introduced between the CAP 10 *ab initio* aircraft and the Magister basic trainer in the *Armée de l'Air* syllabus, the TB 30 is claimed to be suitable for initial selection, primary-basic flying training, and blind flying and navigational training. Stressed to +7*g* and −3·5*g*, the TB 30 meets the requirements of the FAR 23 aerobatic category. The TB 30 is being offered together with the Fouga 90 (see pages 10–11) as a training package by Aérospatiale and is claimed to offer exceptional economy, the piston-engined aircraft covering part of the training spectrum for which more sophisticated aircraft are currently employed.

AÉROSPATIALE TB30 EPSILON

Dimensions: Span, 24 ft 3 in (7,40 m); length, 24 ft 3 in (7,40 m); height, 8 ft 10 in (2,70 m); wing area, 96·87 sq ft (9,00 m²).

AIDC XC-2

Country of Origin: Taiwan (Formosa).
Type: Utility and tactical transport.
Power Plant: Two 1,450 ehp Avco Lycoming T53–L–701A turboprops.
Performance: Max. speed, 265 mph (426 km/h) at 10,000 ft (3 050 m); max. cruise, 253 mph (407 km/h) at 10,000 ft (3 050 m); econ. cruise, 201 mph (324 km/h); initial climb, 1,850 ft/min (9,40 m/sec); service ceiling, 27,400 ft (8 532 m); range with max. payload (8,500 lb/3 855 kg), 357 mls (574 km); range with max. fuel, 1,324 mls (2 130 km).
Weights: Empty equipped, 13,000 lb (5 896 kg); max. take-off, 25,000 lb (11 340 kg).
Accommodation: Crew of three and maximum of 38 passengers in four-abreast seating. Two-section rear loading ramp for freight and paradrops.
Status: The prototype XC-2 was flown for the first time in May 1979. Designed to meet a Nationalist Chinese Air Force requirement for a small tactical transport, the XC-2 is expected to enter production in 1981–82.
Notes: The XC-2 has been developed by the Aero Industry Development Centre and is intended for both civil and military roles. The largest indigenous project undertaken by the AIDC and the first of entirely indigenous design, the XC-2 is designed to operate from short, semi-prepared airstrips and was first projected in 1973. The AIDC is responsible for the part-manufacture and assembly under licence of the F-5E and F-5F, and has built 45 Pazmany PL-1B primary trainers, 118 Bell UH-1H helicopters and 50 T-CH-1 basic trainers (based on the North American T-28).

16

AIDC XC-2

Dimensions: Span, 81 ft 8½ in (24,90 m); length, 64 ft 9 in (19,74 m); height, 25 ft 4 in (7,72 m); wing area, 704 sq ft (65,40 m²).

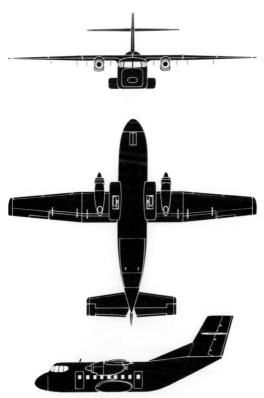

AIRBUS A300B4-100

Country of Origin: International consortium.

Type: Medium-haul commercial transport.

Power Plant: (A300B4-101) Two 51,000 lb (23 130 kg) General Electric CF6-50C turbofans.

Performance: Max. cruise, 578 mph (930 km/h) at 28,000 ft (9 185 m); econ. cruise, 540 mph (869 km/h) at 31,000 ft (9 450 m); long-range cruise, 521 mph (839 km/h) at 33,000 ft (10 060 m); range (with max. payload, no reserve), 2,618 mls (4 213 km); max. range (with 48, 350-lb/21 932-kg payload), 3,994 mls (6 428 km).

Weights: Operational empty, 194,130 lb (85 060 kg); max. take-off, 347,200 lb (157 500 kg).

Accommodation: Crew of three on flight deck with provision for two-man operation. Seating for 220–336 passengers in main cabin in six-, seven- or eight-abreast layouts.

Status: First and second A300Bs flown October 28,1972, and February 5, 1973 (B1 standard), respectively, with third (to B2 standard) flying on June 28, 1973. First A300B4 flown December 26, 1974, and 95 (all versions) delivered by beginning of 1980, when production rate was 2.8 per month against firm orders for 254 (plus 142 options).

Notes: The A300B is manufactured by a consortium of Aérospatiale, British Aerospace and Deutsche Airbus. The A300B2-100 is the basic version, the A300B2-200 having Krueger flaps for improved field performance, and the A300B4-100 is a longer-range model with the Krueger flaps and a centre-section fuel tank, the A300B4-200 having increased gross weight (363,800 lb/165 000 kg). The A300C4 is a convertible passenger/freight variant and the A310 is a short-fuselage, rewinged derivative scheduled to fly in 1981 with service entry in 1983 and for which 61 orders (plus 62 options) had been placed by the beginning of 1980.

18

AIRBUS A300B4-100

Dimensions: Span, 147 ft $1\frac{1}{4}$ in (44,84 m) : length, 175 ft 11 in (53,62 m) ; height, 54 ft 2 in (16,53 m) ; wing area, 2,799 sq ft (260,00 m²).

ANTONOV AN-28 (CASH)

Country of Origin: USSR.

Type: Light STOL general-purpose transport and feederliner.

Power Plant: Two 960 shp Glushenkov TVD-10B turboprops.

Performance: Max. continuous cruising speed, 217 mph (350 km/h); range (with 3,415-lb/1 550-kg payload), 620 mls (1 000 km), (with max. fuel), 805 mls (1 300 km); initial climb rate, 2,360 ft/min (11,99 m/sec).

Weights: Normal loaded, 12,785 lb (5 800 kg); max. take-off, 13,450 lb (6 100 kg).

Accommodation: Flight crew of one or two and up to 18 passengers in high-density configuration, but standard configuration for 15 passengers in three-abreast seating (one to port and two to starboard), the seats folding back against the cabin walls when the aircraft is employed in the freighter or mixed passenger/freight roles. Alternative versions provide for six or seven passengers in an executive transport arrangement and an aeromedical version accommodates six stretchers and a medical attendant.

Status: Initial prototype flown as An-14M in September 1969. A production prototype was tested early in 1974 with 810 hp Isotov TVD-850 turborprops, the aircraft having meanwhile been redesignated An-28, and this was re-engined with Glushenkov TVD-10A engines with which it first flew in April 1975. No series production has been undertaken in the Soviet Union, but licence production is being initiated in Poland by PZL which is expected to commence production deliveries at the end of 1980.

ANTONOV AN-28 (CASH)

Dimensions: Span, 72 ft 2⅛ in (22,00 m); length, 42 ft 6⅞ in (12,98 m); height, 15 ft 1 in (4,60 m).

ANTONOV AN-32 (CLINE)

Country of Origin: USSR.

Type: Commercial freighter and military tactical transport.

Power Plant: Two 4,190 ehp Ivchenko A1-20M turboprops.

Performance: Max. continuous cruise, 317 mph (510 km/h) at 26,250 ft (8 000 m); range (with 13,215-lb/6 000-kg payload and 45 min reserve), 500 mls (800 km), (max. fuel), 1,370 mls (2 200 km); service ceiling, 31,150 ft (9 500 m).

Weights: Max. take-off, 57,270 lb (26 000 kg).

Accommodation: Flight crew of five and 39 passengers on tip-up seats along fuselage sides, 30 fully-equipped paratroops or 24 casualty stretchers and one medical attendant.

Status: The prototype An-32 was flown late 1976. No production had taken place in the Soviet Union at the time of closing for press but negotiations for licence manufacture in India were being finalised late 1979, with initial deliveries from Soviet production 1981–82.

Notes: The An-32 is the latest development in the An-24 (*Coke*) series of transport aircraft and is intended specifically for operation under hot-and-high conditions. Based on the An-26 (*Curl*) and possessing an essentially similar airframe with combined rear-loading ramp/supply drop door, but featuring a 33% increase in available power, the An-32 is capable of operating from unpaved runways and features a 4,400-lb (2 000-kg) capacity electric hoist and a conveyor in the fuselage to assist in the loading of heavy freight. The military version of the An-26 has been widely exported and the An-32 was selected late 1979 to fulfil the Indian Air Force's METAC (Medium Tactical Transport) requirement which calls for 95 aircraft.

ANTONOV AN-32 (CLINE)

Dimensions: Span, 95 ft 9½ in (29,20 m); length, 78 ft 1 in (23,80 m); height, 28 ft 1½ in (8,58 m); wing area, 807·1 sq ft (74,98 m²).

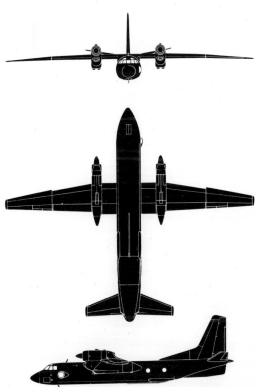

ANTONOV AN-72 (COALER)

Country of Origin: USSR.

Type: Short-haul STOL transport.

Power Plant' Two 14,330 lb (6 500 kg) Lotarev D-36 turbo-fans.

Performance: Max. cruising speed, 447 mph (720 km/h); range with max. payload (16,534 lb/7 500 kg) and 30 min reserves, 620 mls (1 000 km), with max. fuel, 1,990 mls; normal operating altitude, 26,250–32,800 ft (8 000–10 000 m).

Weights: Loaded (for 3,280-ft/1 000-m runway), 58,420 lb (26 500 kg); max. take-off, 67,240 lb (30 500 kg).

Accommodation: Flight crew of two-three and up to 32 passengers on fold-down seats along cabin sides, or 24 casualty stretchers plus one medical attendant. Rear loading ventral ramp with clamshell doors for cargo hold which has overhead hoist and can be provided with roller floor.

Status: First of two prototypes flown on December 22, 1977. No production plans had been revealed at closing for press.

Notes: Similar in concept to the Boeing YC-14 (see 1978 edition) in utilising upper-surface-blowing, engine exhaust gases flowing over the upper wing surfaces and the inboard double-slotted flaps, the An-72 has been designed primarily for use in remote areas and is capable of operating for short, semi-prepared airstrips. Commercial use is likely to be restricted by high operating costs to areas inaccessible to more conventional aircraft and the intended role of the An-72 would appear to be primarily military.

ANTONOV AN-72 (COALER)

Dimensions: Span, 84 ft 9 in (25,83 m); length, 87 ft 2½ in (26,58 m); height, 27 ft 0 in (8,24 m).

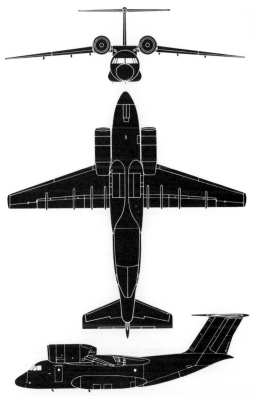

BAe ONE ELEVEN 500

Country of Origin: United Kingdom.

Type: Short- to medium-haul commercial transport.

Power Plant: Two 12,550 lb (5 698 kg) Rolls-Royce Spey 512 DW turbofans.

Performance: Max. cruise, 541 mph (871 km/h) at 21,000 ft (6 400 m); econ. cruise, 461 mph (742 km/h) at 25,000 ft (7 620 m); range with capacity payload (27,090 lb/12 286 kg) and reserves, 1,705 mls (2 744 km), with max. fuel and reserves, 2,165 mls (3 484 km).

Weights: Operational empty, 53,911 lb (24 454 kg); max. take-off, 99,650–104,500 lb (45 200–47 400 kg).

Accommodation: Flight crew of two and up to 119 passengers in main cabin.

Status: Prototype Series 500 (converted from Series 400 development aircraft) flown June 30, 1967, with first production aircraft following on February 7, 1968. Total of 230 ordered (all versions) with Series 475 and Series 500 current production models. One of former and two of latter for Rumania to be delivered 1980–81, to be followed by 22 complete sets of components (both series) for assembly by CNIAR in Rumania by 1985. Thereafter, CNIAR is to produce further 60 Series 475s and 500s at rate of six annually.

Notes: The One-Eleven first flew on August 20, 1963, production models including the physically similar Series 200 and 300 with Spey 506s and Spey 511s respectively, the Series 400 for US operation, the Series 475 combining the fuselage and accommodation of the Series 400 with similar redesigned wing and uprated engines to those of the Series 500 which introduced a lengthened fuselage and wingtip extensions.

BAe ONE-ELEVEN 500

Dimensions: Span, 93 ft 6 in (28,50 m); length, 107 ft 0 in (32,61 m); height, 24 ft 6 in (7,47 m); wing area, 1,031 sq ft (95,78 m²).

BAe 146–100

Country of Origin: United Kingdom.
Type: Short-haul feederliner.
Power Plant: Four 6,700 lb (3 040 kg) Avco Lycoming ALF 502–H turbofans.
Performance: (Estimated) Max. cruise, 490 mph (788 km/h) at 22,000 ft (6 705 m); econ. cruise, 419 mph (674 km/h) at 30,000 ft (9 145 m); range with max. payload (17,942 lb/8 138 kg), 600 mls (1 110 km), with max. fuel plus reserves, 1,704 mls (2 743 km).
Weights: Operational empty, 43,000 lb (19 500 kg); max. take-off, 73,850 lb (33 497 kg).
Accommodation: Flight crew of two and 70 passengers with five-abreast seating or max of 90 with six-abreast seating.
Status: First pre-series BAe 146–100 is scheduled to fly in November 1980, and a further six are expected to fly during the course of 1981. The eighth aircraft scheduled to fly in February 1982 will be the first lengthened BAe 146–200.
Notes: Two production versions of the BAe 146 are currently planned, these being known respectively as the –100 (described and illustrated) and –200 series. The former is intended to operate from short semi-prepared airstrips with minimal ground facilities and the latter, which has an overall length of 93 ft 1 in (28,37 m) and accommodates up to a maximum of 109 passengers at a max. take-off weight of 87,500 lb (39 690 kg), is intended for operation from paved runways only. A military version, the BAe 146M is projected, this being based on the –200 series airframe with a new rear fuselage incorporating aft-loading doors and a ramp, a lowered freight hold floor and a revised undercarriage, each main unit comprising tandem wheels.

28

BAE 146-100

Dimensions: Span, 86 ft 6 in (26,36 m); length, 85 ft 10 in (26,16 m); height, 27 ft 11 in (8,51 m); wing area, 832 sq ft (77,30 m²).

BAe 748 SERIES 2B

Country of Origin: United Kingdom.
Type: Short- to medium-range commercial transport.
Power Plant' Two 2,320 ehp (2,120 shp Rolls-Royce Dart RDa 7 Mk. 536–2 turboprops.
Performance: (At 46,500 lb/21 092 kg) Max. speed, 308 mph (496 km/h) at 16,000 ft (4 875 m); max. cruise, 290 mph (467 km/h) at 15,000 ft (4 570 m); econ. cruise, 270 mph (434 km/h) at 20,000 ft (6 095 m); range (with max. fuel and reserves for 45-min hold and 230-mile/370-km diversion), 1,860 mls (2 993 km), (max. payload and same reserves), 700 mls (1 126 km).
Weights: Typical empty operational, 25,600 lb (11 612 kg); max. take-off, 46,500 lb (21 092 kg).
Accommodation: Normal flight crew of two and standard cabin arrangement for 40 passengers in paired seats.
Status: The first BAe 748 Series 2B was flown on June 22, 1979, this superseding the Series 2A. Total of 345 (all versions) ordered by beginning of 1980 when production rate was nine annually and an order for five (plus an option on five more) from Mountain West was pending. The first customer for the Series 2B was Transkei Airways.
Notes: The Series 2B is the latest production version of the BAe 748, the first prototype of which was flown on June 24, 1960. It differs from the Series 2A (see 1976 edition) that it supplants in having uprated engines with water/methanol injection, extended wingtips, drag reduction modifications and a new fuel management system.

BAE 748 SERIES 2B

Dimensions: Span, 102 ft 6 in (31,23 m); length, 67 ft 0 in (20,42 m); height, 24 ft 10 in (7,57 m); wing area, 828·87 sq ft (77,00 m²).

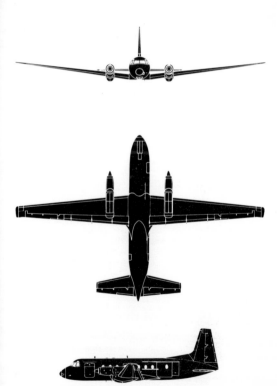

BAe HS 125–700

Country of Origin: United Kingdom.

Type: Light business executive transport.

Power Plant: Two 3,700 lb (1 680 kg) Garrett AiResearch TFE 731-3-1H turbofans.

Performance: High-speed cruise, 495 mph (796 km/h); long-range cruise, 449 mph (722 km/h); range (with 1,200-lb/544-kg payload and 45 min reserve), 2,705 mls (4 355 km); time to 35,000 ft (10 675 m), 19 min; operating altitude, 41,000 ft (12 500 m).

Weights: Typical basic, 13,327 lb (6 045 kg); max. take-off, 24,200 lb (10 977 kg).

Accommodation: Normal flight crew of two and basic lay-out for eight passengers, with alternative layouts for up to 14 passengers.

Status: Series 700 development aircraft flown June 28, 1976, followed by first production aircraft on November 8, 1976. Some 80 HS 125–700s had been delivered by the beginning of 1980, when production rate was three per month and firm orders had been placed for 113 aircraft.

Notes: The HS 125-700 differs from the -600 (see 1976 edition) in that it has supplanted primarily in having turbofans in place of Viper 601 turbojets. Various aerodynamic improvements have also been introduced. Two maritime surveillance versions of the HS 125-700 are on offer, these being the Protector I which retains accommodation for six passengers to provide dual-role capability, and the Protector II which is a dedicated single-role aircraft. Both versions will carry MEL Marec search radar. A successor to the HS 125–700, the HS 125-800 with supercritical wing, lengthened fuselage and, possibly, RB.401 engines, is under consideration.

BAe HS 125-700

Dimensions: Span, 47 ft 0 in (14,32 m); length, 50 ft $8\frac{1}{2}$ in (15,46 m); height, 17 ft 7 in (5,37 m); wing area, 353 sq ft (32,80 m²).

BAe JETSTREAM 31

Country of Origin: United Kingdom.
Type: Light business and utility transport.
Power Plant: Two 940 shp Garrett AiResearch TPE 331—10 turboprops.
Performance: Max. cruise (max. continuous power). 303 mph (488 km/h) at 16,000 ft (4 875 m), (max. cruise power), 291 mph (469 km/h); initial climb, 2,231 ft/min (11.33 m/sec); service ceiling, 31,600 ft (9 480 m); range (with 30 min reserve plus 5% (max. fuel and six passengers), 1,275 mls (2 053 km), (eight passengers), 1,150 mls (1 852 km), (18 passengers), 483 mls (778 km).
Weights: Empty, 7,606 lb (3 450 kg); max. take-off, 14,110 lb (6 400 kg).
Accommodation: Two seats side-by-side on flight deck with 8—10 passengers in main cabin of corporate executive version and optional commuter arrangement for 18 passengers in two-plus-one seating arrangement.
Status: Flight development Jetstream 31 (Jetstream 30) converted from a Series 1 airframe was scheduled to fly March 1980, with first production aircraft following approximately one year later. Customer deliveries are scheduled to commence in 1981.
Notes: The Jetstream 31 is derived from the Handley Page H.P. 137 Jetstream by the Scottish Division of British Aerospace, the original prototype having flown on August 18, 1967. Currently being offered in corporate, commuter and military versions, a production tempo of 25 aircraft annually is anticipated by 1982. At the beginning of 1980, consideration was being given to a 'stretched' version for the commuter market accommodating 25 passengers and a cabin attendant.

BAe JETSTREAM 31

Dimensions: Span, 52 ft 0 in (15,85 m); length, 47 ft 1½ in (14,36 m); height, 10 ft 6 in (3,20 m); wing area, 270 sq ft (25,08 m²).

BAe HARRIER G.R. MK. 3

Country of Origin: United Kingdom.
Type: Single-seat V/STOL strike and reconnaissance fighter.
Power Plant: One 21,500 lb (9 760 kg) Rolls-Royce Pegasus 103 vectored-thrust turbofan.
Performance: Max. speed, 720 mph (1 160 km/h) or Mach 0·95 at 1,000 ft (305 m), with typical external ordnance load, 640–660 mph (1 030–1 060 km) or Mach 0·85–0·87 at 1,000 ft (305 m); cruise, 560 mph (900 km/h) or Mach 0·8 at 20,000 ft (6 096 m); tactical radius for hi-lo-hi mission, 260 mls (418 km), with two 100 Imp gal (455 l) external tanks, 400 mls (644 km).
Weights: Empty, 12,400 lb (5 624 kg); max. take-off (VTO), 18,000 lb (8 165 kg); max. take-off (STO), 23,000+ lb (10 433+ kg); approx. max. take-off, 26,000 lb (11 793 kg).
Armament: Provision for two 30-mm Aden cannon with 130 rpg and up to 5,000 lb (2 268 kg) of ordnance.
Status: First of six pre-production aircraft flown August 31, 1966, with first of 77 G.R. Mk. 1s for RAF following December 28, 1967. Production of G.R. Mk. 1s and 13 T. Mk. 2s (see 1969 edition) for RAF completed. Production of 102 Mk. 50s (equivalent to G.R. Mk. 3) and eight Mk. 54 two-seaters (equivalent to T. Mk. 4) for US Marine Corps, and six Mk. 50s and two Mk. 54s ordered (via the USA) by Spain (by which known as Matador), plus follow-on orders for 13 G.R. Mk. 3s and four T Mk. 4s also completed. Production continuing in 1980 with follow-on orders for 24 Mk. 3s for the RAF, one Mk. 4 for the Royal Navy and two for the Indian Navy, and five Mk. 50s for Spain.
Notes: RAF Harriers have been progressively brought up to G.R. Mk. 3 and T. Mk. 4 standards by installation of Pegasus 103 similar to that installed in Mk. 50 (AV-8A) for USMC.

BAE HARRIER G.R. MK. 3

Dimensions: Span, 25 ft 3 in (7,70 m); length, 45 ft $7\frac{3}{4}$ in (13,91 m); height, 11 ft 3 in (3,43 m); wing area, 201·1 sq ft (18,68 m^2).

BAe HAWK T. MK. 1

Country of Origin: United Kingdom.

Type: Two-seat multi-purpose trainer and light tactical aircraft.

Power Plant: One 5,340 lb (2 422 kg) Rolls-Royce Turboméca RT.172-06-11 Adour 151 turbofan.

Performance: Max. speed, 622 mph (1 000 km/h) at sea level or Mach 0·815, 580 mph (933 km/h) at 36,000 ft (10 970 m) or Mach 0·88; radius of action (HI-LO-HI profile with 5,600-lb/2 540-kg weapons load), 345 mls (560 km), (with 3,000-lb/1 360-kg weapons load and two 100 Imp gal/455 l drop tanks), 645 mls (1 040 km); time to 30,000 ft (9 145 m), 6·1 min; service ceiling, 48,000 ft (14 630 m).

Weights: Empty, 8,040 lb (3 647 kg); loaded (clean), 11,100 lb (5 040 kg); max. take-off, 17,085 lb (7 757 kg).

Armament: (Weapon training) one fuselage centreline and two wing stores stations each stressed for 1,120 lb (508 kg), and (attack) two additional similarly-stressed wing stations. Max. external stores load of 5,600 lb (2 540 kg).

Status: Single pre-production example flown August 21, 1974, first production example flown May 19, 1975, and some 120 delivered by beginning of 1980 against RAF orders for 175 aircraft. Fifty ordered by Finland, eight by Indonesia and 12 by Kenya. Forty-six of those ordered by Finland are to be assembled by Valmet from sets of components supplied by parent company. Production rate of five per month at beginning of 1980.

Notes: Development of combat version being actively pursued at beginning of 1980 when preparations were being made to modify a number of the RAF's Hawk T Mk 1 trainers to carry two AIM-9L Sidewinder air-to-air missiles each with the intention of dispersing these aircraft to operational bases (to be flown by weapons instructors) in an emergency.

BAe HAWK T. MK. 1

Dimensions: Span, 30 ft 9¾ in (9,39 m); length, 38 ft 10⅔ in (11,85 m); height, 13 ft 1 in (4,00 m); wing area, 179·64 sq ft (16,69 m²).

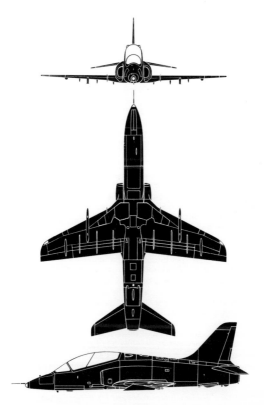

BAe NIMROD M.R. MK. 2

Country of Origin: United Kingdom.

Type: Long-range maritime patrol aircraft.

Power Plant: Four 12,160 lb (5 515 kg) Rolls-Royce RB. 168-20 Spey Mk. 250 turbofans.

Performance: Max. speed, 575 mph (926 km/h); max. transit speed, 547 mph (880 km/h); econ. transit speed, 490 mph (787 km/h); typical ferry range, 5,180–5,755 mls (8 340–9 265 km); typical endurance, 12 hrs.

Weights: Max. take-off, 177,500 lb (80 510 kg); max. overload 192,000 lb (87 090 kg).

Armament: Ventral weapons bay accommodating full range of ASW weapons (Stingray homing torpedoes, mines, depth charges, etc). Provision for two underwing pylons on each side for total of four Aérospatiale AS. 12 ASMs.

Accommodation: Normal operating crew of 12 with two pilots and flight engineer on flight deck and nine navigators and sensor operators in tactical compartment.

Status: First of 38 Nimrod M.R. Mk. 1s flown on June 28, 1968. Completion of this batch in August 1972 followed by delivery of three Nimrod R. Mk. 1s for special electronics reconnaissance, and eight more M.R. Mk. 1s ordered in 1973. Thirty-two Nimrod M.R. Mk. 1s are being progressively brought up to M.R. Mk. 2 standard in a programme scheduled to continue to mid-1984, and the first of these was officially accepted by RAF Strike Command on August 23, 1979.

Notes: Nimrod M.R. Mk. 2 possesses 60 times more computer power than the M.R. Mk. 1, is equipped with the advanced Searchwater maritime radar, an AQS-901 acoustics system compatible with the Barra sonobuoy, and will have EWSM (Electronic Warfare Support Measures) wingtip pods.

BAe NIMROD M.R. Mk. 2

Dimensions: Span, 114 ft 10 in (35,00 m); length, 126 ft 9 in (38,63 m); height, 29 ft 8½ in (9,01 m); wing area, 2,121 sq ft (197,05 m²).

BAe NIMROD A.E.W. MK. 3

Country of Origin: United Kingdom.
Type: Airborne Warning and control system aircraft.
Power Plant' Four 12,160 lb (5 515 kg) Rolls-Royce RB. 168–20 Spey Mk. 250 turbofans.
Performance: No details have been released for publication, but maximum and transit speeds are likely to be generally similar to those of the M.R. Mk. 2, and maximum endurance is in excess of 10 hours. Mission requirement calls for 6–7 hours on station at 29,000–35,000 ft (8 840–10 670 m) at approx. 350 mph (563 km/h) at 750–1,000 mls (1 210–1 600 km) from base.
Weights: No details available.
Accommodation: Flight crew of four and tactical team of six. Tactical team comprises tactical air control officer, communications control officer, EWSM (Electronic Warfare Support Measures) operator and three air direction officers located in the tactical area of the cabin.
Status: Total of 11 Nimrod M.R. Mk. 1 airframes being rebuilt to A.E.W. Mk. 3 standard of which fully representative prototype is scheduled to be rolled out May 1980, with flight testing commencing July 1980. Expected to enter service with the RAF in 1982.
Notes: The Nimrod A.E.W. Mk 3 airborne warning and control system aircraft is equipped with Marconi mission system avionics with identical radar aerial mounted in nose and tail, these being synchronised and each sequentially sweeping through 180 deg in azimuth and providing uninterrupted coverage throughout 360 deg of combined sweep. EWSM pods are located at the wingtips and weather radar is installed in the front of the starboard wing pinion tank. The 11-strong force of Nimrod A.E.W. Mk. 3s will eventually serve with the RAF's No. 8 Squadron.

BAe NIMROD A.E.W. Mk. 3

Dimensions: Span, 115 ft 1 in (35,08 m); length, 137 ft 5½ in (41,76 m); height, 33 ft 0 in (10,06 m); wing area, 2,121 sq ft (197,05 m²).

BAe SEA HARRIER F.R.S. MK. 1

Country of Origin: United Kingdom.
Type: Single-seat V/STOL shipboard multi-role fighter.
Power Plant: One 21,500 lb (9 760 kg) Rolls-Royce Pegasus 104 vectored-thrust turbofan.
Performance: (Estimated) Max. speed, 720 mph (1 160 km/h) at 1,000 ft (305 m) or Mach 0·95, with two Martel ASMs and two Sidewinder AAMs, 640–660 mph (1 030–1 060 km/h) or Mach 0·85–0·87; tactical radius (intercept mission with two 100 Imp gal/455 l drop tanks, two 30-mm cannon and two Sidewinder AAMs), 450 mls (725 km), (strike mission HI-LO-HI profile), 330 mls (480 km).
Weights: Empty, 12,500 lb (5 670 kg); max. STO take-off, 22,500 lb (10 206 kg); max. overload, 25,000 lb (11 339 kg).
Armament: Provision for two (flush-fitting) podded 30-mm Aden cannon with 130 rpg beneath fuselage. Five external hardpoints (one fuselage and four wing) each stressed for 1,000 lb (453,5 kg), with max. external ordnance load for STO (excluding cannon) of 5,000 lb (2 268 kg). Typical loads include two Martel or Harpoon ASMs on inboard wing pylons and two Sidewinder AAMs on outboard pylons.
Status: First Sea Harrier (built on production tooling) flown on August 21, 1978, with deliveries against 34 ordered for Royal Navy commencing in second half of 1979. Six Sea Harriers were ordered late 1979 for delivery to Indian Navy.
Notes: First Sea Harrier squadron, No 700A, was formally commissioned on September 19, 1979.

BAe SEA HARRIER F.R.S. MK. 1

Dimensions: Span, 25 ft 3 in (7,70 m); length, 47 ft 7 in (14,50 m); height, 12 ft 2 in (3,70 m); wing area, 201·1 sq ft (18,68 m²).

BAE-AÉROSPATIALE CONCORDE

Countries of Origin: United Kingdom and France.

Type: Long-range supersonic commercial transport.

Power Plant: Four 38,050 lb (17 259 kg) reheat Rolls-Royce/SNECMA Olympus 593 Mk. 602 turbojets.

Performance: Max. cruise, 1,354 mph (2 179 km/h) at 51,300 ft (15 635 m) or Mach 2·05; range with max. fuel (22,250-lb/10 092-kg payload and FAR reserves), 3,915 mls (6 300 km), with max. payload (28,000 lb/12 700 kg) at Mach 0·93 at 30,000 ft (9 145 m), 3,063 mls (4 930 km), at Mach 2·05, 3,869 mls (6 226 km); initial climb rate, 5,000 ft/min (25,4 m/sec); service ceiling (approx.), 60,000 ft (18 300 m).

Weights: Operational empty, 174,750 lb (79 265 kg); max. take-off, 400,000 lb (181 435 kg).

Accommodation: Normal flight crew of three and one-class seating for 128 passengers. Alternative high-density arrangement for 144 passengers.

Status: First and second prototypes flown March 2 and April 9, 1969, respectively. First of two pre-production aircraft flew December 17, 1971, and the first production example following on December 6, 1973, the last of the French-assembled Concordes flying on December 26, 1978, and the final British-assembled Concorde flying on April 19, 1979. A total of 16 production Concordes was built (Nos 201–216) on separate final assembly lines at Toulouse and Filton (alternate aircraft being assembled in the UK and France), and at the beginning of 1980, five were serving with British Airways and four with Air France, the intention being to augment these fleets with two and one aircraft respectively.

Notes: The Concorde began fare-paying services in January 1976, these being initiated simultaneously by British Airways and Air France. In 1979, Braniff began Concorde services between Washington and Dallas/Fort Worth, leasing the Concordes at the termination of transatlantic flights.

BAE-AÉROSPATIALE CONCORDE

Dimensions: Span, 83 ft 10 in (25,56 m); length, 202 ft $3\frac{3}{8}$ in (61,66 m); height, 37 ft 1 in (11,30 m); wing area, 3,856 sq ft (358,25 m²).

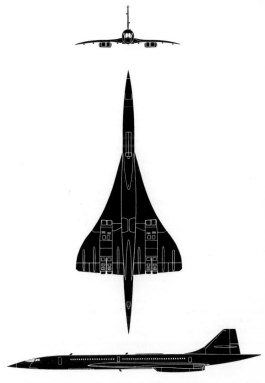

BEECHCRAFT DUCHESS 76

Country of Origin: USA.
Type: Light cabin monoplane.
Power Plant: Two 180 hp Avco Lycoming O-360-A1G6D six-cylinder horizontally-opposed engines.
Performance: Max. speed, 197 mph (317 km/h); max. cruise (at 3,600 lb/1 634 kg), 191 mph (307 km/h) at 6,000 ft (1 830 m); normal cruise, 176 mph (283 km/h) at 10,000 ft (3 050 m); econ. cruise, 172 mph (277 km/h) at 12,000 ft (3 658 m); range at econ. cruise (45 min reserves), 898 mls (1 445 km); initial climb, 1,248 ft/min (6,3 m/sec).
Weights: Empty, 2,446 lb (1 110 kg); max. take-off, 3,900 lb (1 770 kg).
Accommodation: Pilot and three passengers in individual seats, with provision for up to 180 lb (81,6 kg) of baggage in separate compartment.
Status: Prototype flown September 1974, production being initiated in the spring of 1977, and the first production example flying on May 24, 1977. First deliveries were made early 1978, and some 310 had been delivered by the beginning of 1980 with some 160 scheduled for delivery during that year.
Notes: Bearing a close resemblance to the Piper PA-44 Seminole (see pages 182–183), the Duchess embodies handed propellers and honeycomb-bonded wings. It is being marketed through Beech Aero Centers at which it is now becoming the primary twin trainer.

48

BEECHCRAFT DUCHESS 76

Dimensions: Span, 38 ft 0 in (11,58 m); length, 29 ft 0 in (8,84 m); height, 9 ft 6 in (2,89 m); wing area, 181 sq ft (16,81 m²).

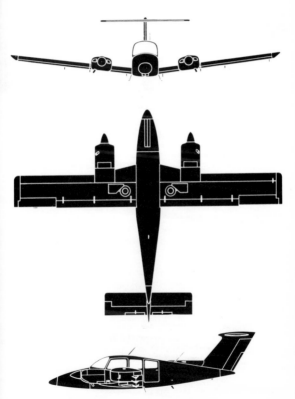

BEECHCRAFT SKIPPER 77

Country of Origin: USA.

Type: Side-by-side two-seat primary trainer.

Power Plant: One 115 hp Avco Lycoming 0-235-L2C four-cylinder horizontally-opposed engine.

Performance: Cruise at 4,500 ft (1 372 m), 121 mph (195 km/h) at 80% power, 112 mph (180 km/h) at 65% power, 107 mph (172 km/h) at 59% power, at 8,500 ft (2 590 m), 110 mph (177 km/h) at 61% power, 105 mph (169 km/h) at 55% power; initial climb, 720 ft/min (3,7 m/sec); service ceiling, 12,900 ft (3 932 m); range (with reserves), 376 mls (605 km) at 80% power at 4,500 ft (1 372 m), 447 mls (719 km) at 8,500 ft (2 590 m) at 61% power.

Weights: Empty, 1,100 lb (499 kg); max. take-off, 1,675 lb (760 kg).

Status: Prototype flown on February 6, 1975, with production prototype following September 1978. Production deliveries commenced April 1979, and approximately 10 per month were being built at the beginning of 1980 when some 65 had been delivered.

Notes: Evolved as a low-cost primary trainer placing emphasis on simplicity of maintenance and low operating cost, the Skipper 77 utilises a NASA-developed high-lift GA(W)-1 wing of tubular-spar concept, and the flaps and ailerons are actuated by torque tubes rather than a conventional cable-and-pulley system. The Skipper closely resembles the competitive Piper PA-38 Tomahawk (see pages 178–179).

BEECHCRAFT SKIPPER 77

Dimensions: Span, 30 ft 0 in (9,14 m); length, 24 ft 0 in (7,32 m); height 7 ft 10¾ in (2,41 m).

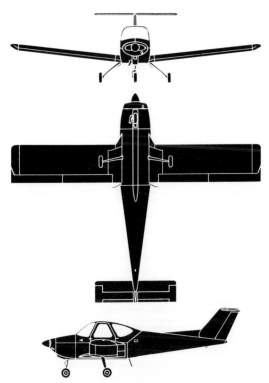

BEECHCRAFT SUPER KING AIR F90

Country of Origin: USA.

Type: Light executive and utility transport.

Power Plant' Two 750 shp Pratt & Whitney PT6A-135 turboprops.

Performance: (At 9,500 lb/4 309 kg) Cruising speed, 307 mph (494 km/h) at 12,000 ft (3 660 m), 300 mph (483 km/h) at 18,000 ft (5 485 m), 289 mph (465 km/h) at 26,000 ft (7 925 m); initial climb (at 10,950 lb/4 967 kg), 2,380 ft/min (12 m/sec); service ceiling, 29,800 ft (9 085 m); range (with reserves), 1,657 mls (2 667 km) at max. cruise power at 26,000 ft (7 925 m), 1,814 mls (2 919 km) at max. range power at 26,000 ft (7 925 m).

Weights: Empty, 6,622 lb (3 004 kg); max. take-off, 10,950 lb (4 967 kg).

Accommodation: Pilot and co-pilot/passenger on flight deck and up to eight passengers in main cabin.

Status: The Super King Air F90, customer deliveries of which commenced in August 1979, as an addition to the King Air range of business aircraft, joining the King Air C90 and B100, and the Super King Air 200 in production. Some 12 Super King Air F90s were scheduled to be delivered by the beginning of 1980, with a further 70 during the course of that year.

Notes: The Super King Air F90 mates the 6–10 passenger capacity of the C90 and E90 King Airs with the performance capability of the 8–15 passenger Super King Air 200 with which it shares as T-type tail arrangement.

BEECHCRAFT SUPER KING AIR F90

Dimensions: Span, 45 ft 10⅘ in (13,99 m); length, 39 ft 9⅜ in (12,13 m); height, 15 ft 1⅕ in (4,60 m); wing area, 279·7 sq ft (25,98 m²).

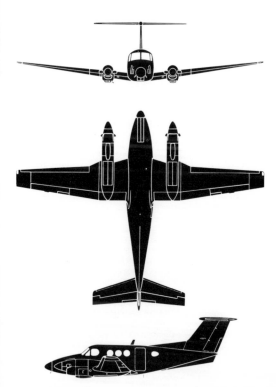

BEECHCRAFT T-34C (TURBINE MENTOR)

Country of Origin: USA.

Type: Tandem two-seat primary trainer.

Power Plant: One 680 shp (derated to 400 shp) Pratt & Whitney (Canada) PT6A-25 turboprop.

Performance: Max. cruise, 213 mph (343 km/h) at sea level, 239 mph (384 km/h) at 10,000 ft (3 050 m); range (5% and 20 min reserve), 787 mls (1 265 km) at 220 mph (354 km/h) at 17,500 ft (5 340 m), 915 mls (1 470 km) at 222 mph (357 km/h) at 25,000 ft (7 625 m); initial climb, 1,430 ft/min (7,27 m/sec).

Weights: Empty equipped, 3,015 lb (1 368 kg); normal loaded, 4,249 lb (1 927 kg).

Status: First of two YT-34Cs flown September 21, 1974, and production continuing at beginning of 1980 for US Navy which had placed orders for 184 aircraft against total requirement for some 278. Export T-34C-1 was delivered to Algeria, Argentina (Navy), Ecuador, Indonesia, Morocco and Peru during 1978.

Notes: Updated derivative of Continental O-470-13-powered Model 45, the T-34C is fitted with a torque-limited PT6A-25 turboprop affording 400 shp, but the T-34C-1 may be fitted with a version of the PT6A-25 derated to 550 shp, wing racks for external ordnance and an armament control system to permit operation as an armament trainer or light counter-insurgency aircraft. With a max. take-off weight of 5,425 lb (2 460 kg), the T-34C-1 has two 600-lb (272-kg) capacity wing inboard stores stations and two 300-lb (136 kg) capacity outboard stations,

BEECHCRAFT T-34C (TURBINE MENTOR)

Dimensions: Span, 33 ft $4\frac{3}{4}$ in (10,18 m); length, 28 ft $8\frac{1}{2}$ in (8,75 m); height, 9 ft $10\frac{7}{8}$ in (3,02 m); wing area, 179·56 sq ft (16,68 m²).

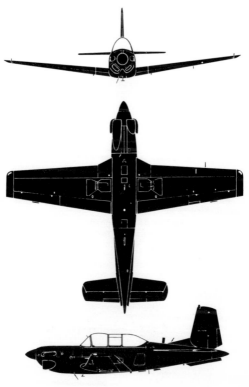

BOEING MODEL 727-200

Country of Origin: USA.

Type: Short- to medium-range commercial transport.

Power Plant: Three 14,500 lb (6 577 kg) Pratt & Whitney JT8D-9 turbofans (with 15,000 lb/6 804 kg JT8D-11s or 15,500 lb/7 030 kg JT8D-15s as options).

Performance: Max. speed, 621 mph (999 km/h) at 20,500 ft (6 250 m); max. cruise, 599 mph (964 km/h) at 24,700 ft (7 530 m); econ. cruise, 570 mph (917 km/h) at 30,000 ft (9 145 m); range with 26,400-lb (11 974-kg) payload and normal reserves, 2,850 mls (4 585 km), with max. payload (41,000 lb/18 597 kg), 1,845 mls (2 970 km).

Weights: Operational empty (basic), 97,525 lb (44 235 kg), (typical), 99,000 lb (44 905 kg); max. take-off, 208,000 lb (94 347 kg).

Accommodation: Crew of three on flight deck and six-abreast seating for 163 passengers in basic arrangement with max. seating for 189 passengers.

Status: First Model 727-100 flown February 9, 1963, with first delivery (to United) following October 29, 1963. Model 727-200 flown July 27, 1967, with first delivery (to Northeast) on December 11, 1967. Deliveries from mid-1972 have been of the so-called "Advanced 727-200" (to which specification refers and illustrations apply) and sales of Model 727s had exceeded 1,720 at the beginning of 1980, with 1,550 delivered and production running at 11 aircraft monthly.

Notes: The Model 727-200 is a "stretched" version of the 727-100 (see 1972 edition). Deliveries of the "Advanced 727" with JT8D-17 engines of 16,000 lb (7 257 kg), permitting an increase of 3,500 lb (1 587 kg) in payload, began (to Mexicana) in June 1974. The 1,282nd Model 727 delivered in August 1977 was Boeing's 3,000th jetliner. Almost two-thirds of all Model 727 sales have been of -200 series aircraft.

BOEING MODEL 727-200

Dimensions: Span, 108 ft 0 in (32,92 m); length, 153 ft 2 in (46,69 ml); height, 34 ft 0 in (10,36 m); wing area, 1,560 sq ft (144,92 m²).

BOEING MODEL 737-200

Country of Origin: USA.

Type: Short-haul commercial transport.

Power Plant: Two 14,500 lb (6 577 kg) Pratt & Whitney JT8D-9 turbofans.

Performance: Max. speed, 586 mph (943 km/h) at 23,500 ft (7 165 m); max. cruise (at 90,000 lb/40 823 kg), 576 mph (927 km/h) at 22,600 ft (6 890 m); econ. cruise, 553 mph (890 km/h) at 30,000 ft (9 145 m); range (max. fuel and reserves), 2,530 mls (4 075 km), (max. payload of 34,790 lb/ 15 780 kg and reserves), 2,370 mls (3 815 km).

Weights: Operational empty, 60,210 lb (27 310 kg); max. take-off, 115,500 lb (52 390 kg).

Accommodation: Flight crew of two and up to 130 passengers in six-abreast seating with alternative arrangement for 115 passengers.

Status: Model 737 initially flown on April 9, 1967, with first deliveries (737-100 to Lufthansa) same year. Stretched 737-200 flown on August 8, 1967, with deliveries (to United) in 1968. Total sales were 745 (including 19-200s delivered to USAF as T-43A navigational trainers—see 1975 edition) by the beginning of 1980, with 620 delivered and production running at three monthly.

Notes: All aircraft delivered since May 1971 have been completed to the so-called "Advanced 737-200/C/QC" standard embodying improvements in range and short-field performance. JT8D-15 or -17 engines are optional and a max. take-off weight option of 117,000 lb (53 070 kg) is available, while a 128,600 lb (58 332 kg) take-off weight was expected to be certificated early in 1979, with a commensurate payload increase, this having called for strengthening in a number of areas.

BOEING MODEL 737-200

Dimensions: Span, 93 ft 0 in (28,35 m); length, 100 ft 0 in (30,48 m); height, 37 ft 0 in (11,28 m); wing area, 980 sq ft (91,05 m²).

BOEING MODEL 747-200B

Country of Origin: USA.

Type: Long-range large-capacity commercial transport.

Power Plant: Four 47,000 lb (21 320 kg) Pratt & Whitney JT9D-7W turbofans.

Performance: Max. speed at 600,000 lb (272 155 kg), 608 mph (978 km/h) at 30,000 ft (9 150 m); long-range cruise, 589 mph (948 km/h) at 35,000 ft (10 670 m); range with max. fuel and FAR reserves, 7,080 mls (11 395 km), with 79,618-lb (36 114-kg) payload, 6,620 mls (10 650 km); cruise ceiling, 45,000 ft (13 715 m).

Weights: Operational empty, 361,216 lb (163 844 kg); max. take-off, 775,000 lb (351 540 kg).

Accommodation: Normal flight crew of three and basic accommodation for 66 first-class and 308 economy-class passengers. Alternative layouts for 447 or 490 economy-class passengers nine- and 10-abreast respectively.

Status: First Model 747-100 flown on February 9, 1969, and first commercial services (by Pan American) inaugurated January 22, 1970. The first Model 747-200 (747B), the 88th aircraft off the assembly line, flown October 11, 1970. Orders (all versions) had passed 510 by the beginning of 1980, with 415 delivered and production seven monthly.

Notes: Principal versions are the -100 and -200 series, the latter having greater fuel capacity and increased maximum take-off weight, convertible passenger/cargo and all-cargo versions of the -200 series being designated 747-200C and 747-200F. The first production example of the latter flew on November 30, 1971. Deliveries of the Model 747SR, a short-range version of the 747-100 (to Japan Air Lines), began September 1973. The 747-200B was flown on June 26, 1973 with 51,000 lb (23 133 kg) General Electric CF6-50D engines, and the 52,500 lb (23 810 kg) CF6-50E and the 52,000 lb (23 585 kg) Rolls-Royce RB.211-524 are offered as options.

BOEING MODEL 747-200B

Dimensions: Span, 195 ft 8 in (59,64 m); length, 231 ft 4 in (70,51 m); height, 63 ft 5 in (19,33 m); wing area, 5,685 sq ft (528,15 m²).

BOEING MODEL 747SP

Country of Origin: USA.

Type: Long-haul commercial transport.

Power Plant: Four 46,950 lb (21 296 kg) Pratt & Whitney JT9D-7A turbofans.

Performance: Max. cruise, 594 mph (957 km/h) at 35,000 ft (10 670 m); econ. cruise, 570 mph (918 km/h) at 35,000 ft (10 670 m); long-range cruise, 555 mph (893 km/h); range (with max. payload of 97,080 lb/44 034 kg), 6,620 mls (10 650 km), (with max. fuel and 30,000-lb/13 608-kg payload), 9,570 mls (15 400 km).

Weights: Operational empty, 315,000 lb (140 878 kg); max. take-off, 660,000 lb (299 370 kg).

Accommodation: Flight crew of three and basic accommodation for 28 first-class and 288 economy-class passengers. Max. high-density arrangement for 360 passengers in 10-abreast seating.

Status: First production Model 747SP flown July 4, 1975, with first customer deliveries (to Pan Am) following early 1976. Thirty-five ordered by nine operators by beginning of 1980.

Notes: The SP (Special Performance) version of the Model 747 embodies a reduction in overall length of 47 ft 7 in (14,30 m) and retains a 90% commonality of components with the standard Model 747 (see pages 60–61). The Model 747SP is intended primarily for operation over long-range routes where traffic densities are insufficient to support the standard model. Apart from having a shorter fuselage, the Model 747SP has taller vertical tail surfaces with a double-hinged rudder and new trailing-edge flaps. CAAC became 60th Boeing 747 customer on December 16, 1978, with an order for three (and option on two more) 747SPs.

BOEING MODEL 747SP

Dimensions: Span, 195 ft 8 in (59,64 m); length, 184 ft 9 in (56,31 m); height, 65 ft 5 in (19,94 m); wing area, 5,685 sq ft (528,15 m²).

BOEING E-3A SENTRY

Country of Origin: USA.

Type: Airborne warning and control system aircraft.

Power Plant: Four 21,000 lb (9 525 kg) Pratt & Whitney TF33-PW-100A turbofans.

Performance: (At max. weight) Average cruising speed, 479 mph (771 km/h) at 28,900–40,100 ft (8 810–12 220 m); average loiter speed, 376 mph (605 km/h) at 29,000 ft (8 840 m); time on station (unrefuelled) at 1,150 mls (1 850 km) from base, 6 hrs, (with one refuelling), 14·4 hrs; ferry range (crew reduced to four members), 5,034 mls (8 100 km) at 475 mph (764 km/h).

Weights: Empty, 170,277 lb (77 238 kg); normal loaded, 214,300 lb (97 206 kg); max. take-off, 325,000 lb (147 420 kg).

Accommodation: Operational crew of 17 comprising flight crew of four, systems maintenance team of four, a battle commander and an air defence operations team of eight.

Status: First of two (EC-137D) development aircraft flown February 9, 1972, two pre-production E-3As following in 1975. Seventeen Sentries delivered by beginning of 1980 when procurement of three per year was planned through 1983 to provide total of 31 aircraft. Deliveries of 18 for NATO (excluding UK) operation scheduled to commence 1982, with full deployment following in 1984.

BOEING E-3A SENTRY

Dimensions: Span, 145 ft 9 in (44,42 m); length, 152 ft 11 in (46,61 m); height, 42 ft 5 in (12,93 m); wing area, 2,892 sq ft (268,67 m²).

BOEING E-4B

Country of Origin: USA.
Type: Airborne command post aircraft.
Power Plant: Four 52,500 lb (23 814 kg) General Electric F103-GE-100 turbofans.
Performance: Generally similar to that of commercial Model 747-200B (e.g., max. speed, 608 mph/978 km/h at 30,000 ft/ 9 150 m; long-range cruise, 589 mph/948 km/h at 35,000 ft/ 10 670 m). Intended for long-endurance missions, the E-4B is equipped for in-flight refuelling and is theoretically capable of remaining airborne for 72 hours.
Weights: Max. take-off, 780,000 lb (353 808 kg).
Accommodation: The E-4B accommodates two complete flight crews with rest area on upper deck and an operating crew of some 50 personnel on the main deck. This is divided into six areas: the National Command Authority's working area, conference room, briefing room, battle staff working area, communications control centre and rest area. Lobe areas beneath the main deck house a technical control facility and a limited onboard maintenance storage area.
Status: Delivery of the first E-4B was taken in August 1975, but this aircraft was not flown with full electronic equipment until June 10, 1978, and is scheduled to achieve operational capability with USAF Strategic Air Command early in 1980. This was preceded by three E-4A interim airborne command posts, which are to be retrofitted to E-4B standard from 1981, and is being followed by two additional E-4Bs to provide total fleet of six aircraft in the mid 'eighties.
Notes: Radome on upper forward fuselage houses a satellite communications antenna.

BOEING E-4B

Dimensions: Span, 195 ft 8 in (59,64 m); length, 231 ft 4 in (70,51 m); height, 63 ft 5 in (19,33 m); wing area, 5,685 sq ft (528,14 m²).

CANADAIR CL-600 CHALLENGER

Country of Origin: Canada.
Type: Light business executive transport.
Power Plant: Two 7,500 lb (3 405 kg) Avco Lycoming ALF 502L turbofans.
Performance: High-speed cruise, 561 mph (903 km/h) or Mach 0·85; normal cruise, 547 mph (882 km/h) or Mach 0·83; long-range cruise, 502 mph (807 km/h) or Mach 0·75; ceiling, 47,000 ft (14 935 m); range (with IFR reserves), 3,800 miles (6 115 km) at Mach 0·80.
Weights: Typical operational empty, 20,220 lb (9 172 kg); max. take-off, 36,000 lb (16 329 kg).
Accommodation: Basic flight crew of two and executive lay-outs for 8–14 passengers.
Status: First Challenger (built on production jigs) flown on November 8, 1978, with second and third following on March 17 and 14 July 1979 respectively. Total of 123 on order at beginning of 1980, with first customer deliveries scheduled for first quarter of the year, a production rate of up to seven per month planned for early 1981.
Notes: During 1979, Canadair announced preliminary details of a stretched version, the Challenger E, which will be available for delivery from mid-1983. This will have an 8 ft 9 in (2,67 m) fuselage stretch to permit accommodation of some 40 passengers four-abreast in a commuter liner version and will be powered by two 8,650 lb (3 924 kg) General Electric CF34 high bypass turbofans, maximum take-off weight being 48,000 lb (21 792 kg). Challengers delivered after September 1980 will feature a 345-mile (556-km) range increase.

CANADAIR CL-600 CHALLENGER

Dimensions: Span, 61 ft 10 in (18,85 m); length, 88 ft 5 in (20,85 m); height, 20 ft 8 in (6,30 m); wing area, 450 sq ft (41,81 m²).

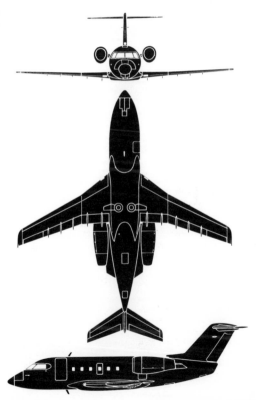

CASA C-101 AVIOJET

Country of Origin: Spain.

Type: Two-seat basic and advanced trainer.

Power Plant: One 3,500 lb (1 588 kg) Garrett AiResearch TFE 731-2-2J turbofan.

Performance: (At 10,362 lb/4 700 kg) Max. speed, 479 mph (770 km/h) or Mach 0·7 at 28,000 ft (8 535 m), 404 mph (650 km/h) or Mach 0·53 at sea level; time to 25,000 ft (7 620 m), 12 min; service ceiling, 41,000 ft (12 495 m); range (internal fuel at 11,540 lb/5 235 kg), 2,485 mls (4 000 km); max. climb (at 10,362 lb/4 700 kg), 3,350 ft/min (17 m/sec).

Weights: Basic operational empty, 6,790 lb (3 080 kg); loaded (pilot training mission with outer wing tanks empty), 10,362 lb (4 700 kg), (with max. internal fuel), 11,540 lb (5 235 kg); max. take-off, 12,346 lb (5 600 kg).

Armament: Seven external stores stations (six wing and one fuselage) for maximum of 3,307 lb (1 500 kg) of ordnance. Provision is made for a semi-recessed pod beneath the aft cockpit for a 30-mm cannon or two 7,62-mm Miniguns. Warload options include four Mk. 83 or six Mk. 82 bombs, or four AGM-65 Maverick missiles.

Status: Four prototypes of which first flown on June 29, 1977, and last on April 17, 1978. Sixty ordered by Spanish Air Force in March 1978, of which first scheduled to be delivered October 1979 with last being delivered March 1981.

Notes: The Aviojet will replace the Saeta series in service from 1980.

70

CASA C-101 AVIOJET

Dimensions: Span, 34 ft $9\frac{3}{8}$ in (10,60 m); length, 40 ft $2\frac{1}{4}$ in (12,25 m); height, 13 ft 11 in (4,25 m); wing area, 215·3 sq ft (20,00 m²).

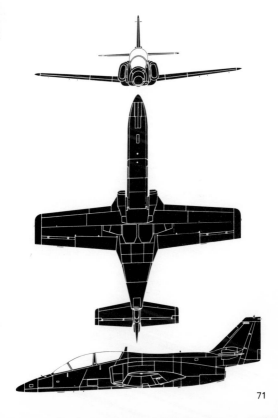

CESSNA CUTLASS RG

Country of Origin: USA.

Type: Four-seat light cabin monoplane.

Power Plan One 180 hp Avco Lycoming 0-360-F1A6 six-cylinder horizontally-opposed engine.

Performance: Max. speed, 167 mph (269 km/h at sea level; cruise (75% power), 161 mph (259 km/h) at 9,000 ft (2 745 m); initial climb, 800 ft/min (6,06 m/sec); service ceiling, 16,800 ft (5 120 m); max. range, 967 mls (1 556 km) at 10,000 ft (3 050 m).

Weights: Empty, 1,558 lb (507 kg); max. take-off, 2,650 lb (1 202 kg).

Accommodation: Four seats in two pairs with baggage space (120 lb/54 kg capacity) aft of rear seats.

Status: The Cutlass was announced in the autumn of 1979, and customer deliveries were scheduled for the beginning of 1980.

Notes: The Cutlass is effectively a retractable undercarriage version of the well-known Model 172, more than 30,000 examples of which have been built (2,161 of all models being delivered in 1978 and production averaging 155 monthly in 1979). The retractable undercarriage of the Cutlass is similar to that already proven on the more powerful Skylane RG and integral wing fuel tanks similar to those introduced by the Hawk XP version of the Model 172. The Model 172 series, of which the Cutlass is the latest addition, was originally introduced in 1955, and was, itself, initially a Model 170 (first introduced in 1948) with a nosewheel undercarriage and revised tail surfaces.

CESSNA CUTLASS RG

Dimensions: Span, 35 ft 10 in (10,92 m); length, 27 ft 5 in (8,36 m); height, 8 ft 9½ in (2,68 m); wing area, 174 sq ft (16,20 m²).

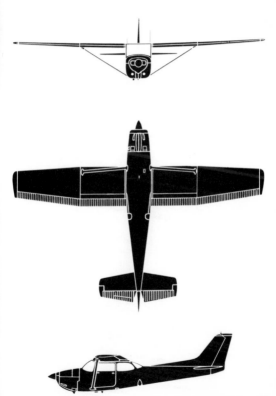

CESSNA CITATION II

Country of Origin: USA.

Type: Light business executive transport.

Power Plant: Two 2,500 lb (1 135 kg) Pratt & Whitney (Canada) JT15D-4 turbofans.

Performance: Max. cruise, 420 mph (676 km/h) at 25,400 ft (7 740 m); range cruise, 380 mph (611 km/h) at 43,000 ft (13 105 m); range (with eight passengers and 45 min reserve), 2,080 mls (3 347 km) at 380 mph (611 km/h); initial climb, 3,500 ft/min (17,8 m/sec); time to 41,000 ft (12 495 m), 34 min; max. cruise altitude, 43,000 ft (13 105 m).

Weights: Typical empty equipped, 6,960 lb (3 160 kg); max. take-off, 12,500 lb (5 675 kg).

Accommodation: Normal flight crew of two on separate flight deck and up to 10 passengers in main cabin.

Status: Two prototypes of Citation II flown January 31 and April 28, 1977, respectively, with first customer deliveries commencing late March 1978, with 100th delivered in September 1979, when production rate was 10 monthly (plus five Citation Is). Some 170 Citation Is and IIs are expected to be delivered during 1980.

Notes: The Citation II is a stretched (4 ft/1,22 m longer cabin) version of the original Citation, with a higher aspect ratio wing, uprated engines and increased fuel capacity, and is being manufactured in parallel with the Citation I and I/SP (the latter catering for single-pilot operation) with similar accommodation to the first Citation, JT15D-1A turbofans and a 47 ft 1 in/14,36 m wing. Citation I deliveries began in February 1977.

CESSNA CITATION II

Dimensions: Span, 51 ft 8 in (15,76m); length, 47 ft 3 in (14,41 m); height, 14 ft 11 in (4,55 m).

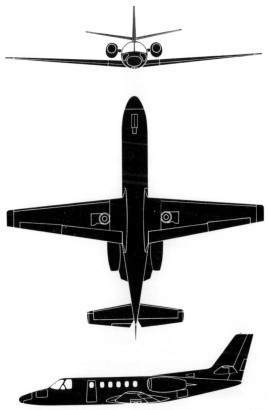

75

CESSNA CITATION III

Country of Origin: USA.
Type: Light business executive transport.
Power Plant: Two 3,700 lb (1 680 kg) Garrett AiResearch TFE 731-3-100S turbofans.
Performance: Cruising speed (at 13,700 lb/6 214 kg), 540 mph (869 km/h) at 33,000 ft (10 060 m); time (at 17,000 lb/7 711 kg) to 35,000 ft (10 670 m), 11 min, to 41,000 ft (12 495 m), 18 min, to 43,000 ft (13 105 m), 28 min; range (four passengers), 2,875 mls (4 626 km), (with 10 passengers), 2,190 mls (3 524 km).
Weights: Operational empty, 9,325 lb (4 230 kg); max. take-off, 19,500 lb (8 845 kg).
Accommodation Normal flight crew of two on separate flight deck and up to 13 passengers in main cabin.
Status: The engineering prototype Citation III was flown for the first time on May 30, 1979, with customer deliveries scheduled to commence October 1981. First production Citation III is scheduled to be completed during first quarter of 1981.
Notes: The Citation III possesses no commonality with the Citation II (see pages 74–75) despite its name, and is offered in basic (described above) and extended range versions, the latter augmenting the integral wing tanks with a fuselage tank which provides the ability to carry two crew members, six passengers and their baggage over a distance of 3,453 mls (5 557 km). A second flying prototype was scheduled to join the test programme early 1980.

CESSNA CITATION III

Dimensions: Span, 53 ft 3½ in (16,30 m); length, 55 ft 6 in (16,90 m); height, 17 ft 3½ in (5,30 m); wing area, 312 sq ft (29,00 m²).

DASSAULT-BREGUET ATLANTIC NG

Country of Origin: France.

Type: Long-range maritime patrol aircraft.

Power Plant: Two 6,105 ehp Rolls-Royce (SNECMA) Tyne TRy 20 Mk. 21 turboprops.

Performance: (Estimated) Max. speed, 368 mph (593 km/h) at sea level, 409 mph (658 km/h) at 26,245 ft (8 000 m); max. continuous cruise, 348 mph (560 km/h) at 19,685 ft (6 000 m); patrol speed, 196 mph (315 km/h); max. endurance, 16 hrs at 207 mph (333 km/h) at 19,685 ft (6 000 m); typical missions, 8-hr patrol at 690 mls (1 110 km) from base or 5-hr patrol at 1,150 mls (1 850 km) from base.

Weights: Empty equipped, 55,280 lb (25 075 kg); max. loaded, 99,206 lb (45 000 kg); max. overload, 101,852 lb (46 200 kg).

Armament: Ventral weapons bay accommodating full range of ASW weapons (homing torpedoes, mines, depth charges), plus four underwing pylons for AM 39 air-to-surface missiles.

Accommodation: Normal operating crew of 12 with two pilots and flight engineer on flight deck, and nine navigational personnel and systems operators in nose, main tactical and rear compartments.

Status: Pre-prototype (Atlantic NG No 001) converted from definitive Atlantic prototype (No 04) initiated NG test programme spring 1979. Two definitive prototypes, NG No 01 and No 02 (converted from Nos 42 and 69 production Atlantics) to fly May 1981 and early 1982 respectively. Production deliveries against French Navy requirement for 42 aircraft scheduled to commence early 1985.

Notes: Atlantic NG (*Nouvelle Génération*) is a modernised version of Atlantic, production of which terminated in 1973 after completion of 87 series aircraft.

DASSAULT-BREGUET ATLANTIC NG

Dimensions: Span, 119 ft 1¼ in (36,30 m); length, 104 ft 1½ in (31,74 m); height, 33 ft 1¾ in (11,35 m); wing area, 1,291·7 sq ft (120 m²).

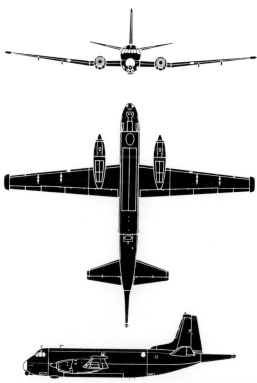

DASSAULT-BREGUET FALCON 20H

Country of Origin: France.

Type: Light business executive transport.

Power Plant: Two 5,300 lb (2 405 kg) Garrett AiResearch ATF 3-6-2C turbofans.

Performance: Max. cruise, 540 mph (870 km/h) at 33,000 ft (10 060 m); range (eight passengers and IFR reserves), 1,785 mls (2 872 km) at max. cruise, (with 45-min UFR reserve), 2,900 mls (4 666 km) at long-range cruise at 37,000 ft (11 275 m).

Weights: Empty, 17,700 lb (8 029 kg); max. take-off, 31,000 lb (14 060 kg).

Accommodation: Crew of two on flight deck and normal seating for 8–10 passengers in main cabin, or maximum of 12–14 passengers with seats at reduced pitch and no tables between forward pairs of seats.

Status: Intermediate prototype, the Falcon 20FH (retaining CF 700 engines of Falcon 20F), flown on April 24, 1979, with full Falcon 20H prototype scheduled to be certificated in second half of 1980. Current planning calls for replacement in production of Falcon 20F by Falcon 20H in late 1981.

Notes: The Falcon 20H takes advantage of the development of a new fuel system for the larger Falcon 50 (see pages 82–83) combined with the ATF 3-6-2C installation engineered for the Falcon 20G Guardian (see 1979 edition) to produce an aircraft with 42 per cent more range than the current Falcon 20F with the same payload. The additional fuel capacity is provided by a single tank integral with the fuselage structure behind the rear pressure bulkhead. The equivalent maritime surveillance Falcon 20G (HU-25A Guardian) is to be delivered to the US Coast Guard from July 1980. Five Falcon 20 Hs have been ordered for maritime surveillance by the French Navy.

DASSAULT-BREGUET FALCON 20H

Dimensions: Span, 53 ft 5¾ in (16,30 m); length, 56 ft 2⅞ in (17,14 m); height, 17 ft 5 in (5,32 m); wing area, 449·93 sq ft (41,80 m²).

DASSAULT-BREGUET FALCON 50

Country of Origin: France.

Type: Light business executive transport.

Power Plant: Three 3,700 lb (1 680 kg) Garrett AiResearch TFE 731-3 turbofans.

Performance: Max. cruise, 560 mph (900 km/h) at 30,000 ft (9 145 m), or Mach 0·83; long-range cruise, 495 mph (792 km/h) at 37,000 ft (11 275 m), or Mach 0·75; range (with eight passengers and 45 min plus 173-mile/288-km reserve), 3,800 mls (6 115 km) at long-range cruise, 3,454 mls (5 560 km) at 528 mph (850 km/h), or Mach 0·8; max. operating altitude, 41,000 ft (12 500 m).

Weights: Empty equipped, 19,840 lb (9 000 kg); max. take-off, 37,480 lb (17 000 kg).

Accommodation: Flight crew of two and various cabin arrangements for six to ten passengers.

Status: First prototype flown November 7, 1976, with second flown on February 16, 1978, and the first pre-series aircraft following on June 13, 1978. First production delivery (to Falcon Jet Corp) was made on March 30, 1979, and seven production aircraft had been delivered by the beginning of 1980, when orders totalled 117 aircraft and production was building to four monthly.

Notes: Subsequent to initial flight testing, the first prototype Falcon 50 was modified to incorporate a supercritical wing having the same planform as the original wing. The first production aircraft established five (C-1H class) world records on March 31, 1979 during non-stop ferry flight Bordeaux-Teterboro.

DASSAULT-BREGUET FALCON 50

Dimensions: Span, 62 ft 2⅖ in (18,96 m); length, 60 ft 9 in (18,52 m); height, 22 ft 10⅖ in (6,97 m); wing area, 504·13 sq ft (46,83 m²).

DASSAULT-BREGUET MIRAGE F1

Country of Origin: France.

Type: Single-seat multi-purpose fighter.

Power Plant: One 11,023 lb (5 000 kg) dry and 15,873 lb
(7 200 kg) reheat SNECMA Atar 9K-50 turbojet.

Performance: Max. speed (clean), 915 mph (1 472 km/h)
or Mach 1·2 at sea level, 1,450 mph (2 335 km/h) or Mach
2·2 at 39,370 ft (12 000 m); range cruise, 550 mph (885
km/h) at 29,530 ft (9 000 m); range with max. external
fuel, 2,050 mls (3 300 km), with max. external combat load
of 8,818 lb (4 000 kg), 560 mls (900 km), with external
combat load of 4,410 lb (2 000 kg), 1,430 mls (2 300 km);
service ceiling, 65,600 ft (20 000 m).

Weights: Empty, 16,314 lb (7 400 kg); loaded (clean),
24,030 lb (10 900 kg); max. take-off, 32,850 lb (14 900 kg).

Armament: Two 30-mm DEFA cannon and (intercept) 1-3
Matra 530 Magic and two AIM-9 Sidewinder AAMs.

Status: First of four prototypes flown December 23, 1966.
First production for *Armée de l'Air* flown February 15,
1973. Production rate of six per month at beginning of 1980.
Licence manufacture is being undertaken in South Africa. Firm
orders totalled more than 550 aircraft by beginning of 1980
including Greece, 40 (F1CG), Kuwait, 20 (18 F1CK and two
F1BK), Libya, 38 (32 F1ED and six F1BD), Iraq, 36 (inc. four
F1B), Morocco, 50 (F1CH), South Africa, 48 (16 F1CZ and
32 F1AZ), Spain, 73 (F1CE), and Ecuador, 18. The *Armée de
l'Air* planned total procurement of 214.

Notes: Production versions currently comprise F1A and F1E
for ground attack role, the former for VFR operations only, the
F1BD tandem two-seat conversion trainer, 14 of which have
been ordered by the *Armée de l'Air*, and the F1C interceptor.

DASSAULT-BREGUET MIRAGE F1

Dimensions: Span, 27 ft $6\frac{3}{4}$ in (8,40 m); length, 49 ft $2\frac{1}{2}$ in (15,00 m); height, 14 ft 9 in (4,50 m); wing area, 269·098 sq ft (25 m²).

DASSAULT-BREGUET MIRAGE 2000

Country of Origin: France.

Type: Single-seat multi-role fighter.

Power Plant: One 19,840 lb (9 000 kg) reheat SNECMA M53-5 turbofan (bypass turbojet).

Performance: Max. attainable speed, 1,550 mph (2 495 km/h) above 36,090 ft (11 000 m) or Mach 2·35; max. sustained speed, 1,452 mph (2 336 km/h) or Mach 2·0; time to Mach 2·0 at 49,200 ft (15 000 m) from brakes release (with four AAMs), 4 min; max. climb rate, 49,000 ft/min (249 m/sec); operational ceiling, 65,000 ft (19 810 m); tactical radius (four AAMs and two 374 Imp gal/1 700 l drop tanks), 435 mls (700 km).

Weights: Combat, 19,840 lb (9 000 kg); max. take-off, 33,070 lb (15 000 kg).

Armament: Two 30-mm DEFA 554 cannon and (air superiority) two Matra 550 Magic and two Matra Super 530D AAMs, or (strike) up to 11,000 lb (5 000 kg) of ordnance on nine external stations (four beneath wings and five beneath fuselage).

Status: First and second prototypes flown March 10 and September 18, 1978, respectively, with third prototype flown on April 26, 1979. The fourth and fifth (two-seat) prototypes are scheduled to fly during 1980, with first production aircraft at beginning of 1982, four having been ordered in the Fiscal 1979 budget, with 23 expected to be ordered in 1980, 43 in 1981 and 44 in 1982.

Notes: *Armée de l'Air* has a requirement for total of 200 Mirage 2000s for the air defence role with probable follow-on of similar quantity configured for interdiction and reconnaissance.

DASSAULT-BREGUET MIRAGE 2000

Dimensions: Span, 29 ft 6⅓ in (9,00 m); length, 50 ft 3½ in (15,33 m); wing area, 441·3 sq ft (41,00 m²).

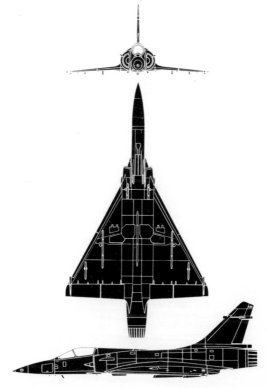

DASSAULT-BREGUET SUPER MIRAGE 4000

Country of Origin: France.
Type: Single-seat multi-role fighter.
Power Plant: Two 18,720 lb (8 500 kg) reheat SNECMA M53-2 turbofans (to be replaced by 19,840 lb/9 000 kg M53-5s).
Performance: (Estimated) Max. sustained speed, 1,452 mph (2 336 km/h) or Mach 2·2 above 36,090 ft (11 000 m), 915 mph (1 472 km/h) or Mach 1·2 at sea level; max. climb rate, 50,000 ft/min (254 m/sec); operational ceiling, 65,000 ft (19 810 m).
Weights: (Estimated) Loaded (clean), 37,500 lb (17 000 kg); max. take-off, 45,000 lb (20 410 kg).
Armament: Two 30-mm DEFA 554 cannon and up to 15,000 lb (6 804 kg) of ordnance on nine external stations (four wing and five fuselage).
Status: Sole prototype Super Mirage 4000 flown on March 9, 1979.
Notes: Developed as a private venture, the Super Mirage 4000 is optimised for the deep penetration role but is also suitable for intercept and air superiority missions, and is most closely comparable with the McDonnell Douglas F-15 Eagle. It closely resembles the Mirage 2000 (see page 86–87) in aerodynamic, structural and systems layout, sharing with the smaller aircraft such features as fly-by-wire controls, artificial stability, leading-edge flaps and the use of carbon-fibre composites, components using these materials including the fin and rudder, the elevons and the canard surfaces attached to the outer sides of the intake ducts. The *Armée de l'Air* currently possesses no requirement for an aircraft in the category of the Super Mirage.

DASSAULT-BREGUET SUPER MIRAGE 4000

Dimensions: Span, 39 ft 4½ in (12,00 m); length, 61 ft 4¼ in (18,70 m); wing area, 786 sq ft (73,00 m²).

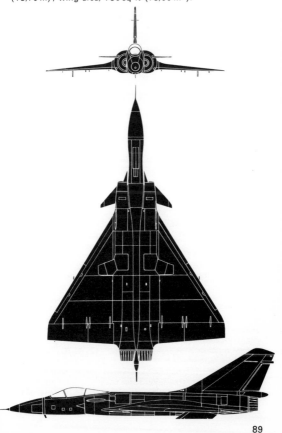

DASSAULT-BREGUET/DORNIER
ALPHA JET

Countries of Origin: France and Federal Germany.
Type: Two-seat basic-advanced trainer and light tactical aircraft.
Power Plant: Two 2,975 lb (1 350 kg) SNECMA-Turboméca Larzac 04-C5 turbofans.
Performance: Max. speed, 622 mph (1 000 km/h) at sea level or Mach 0·816, 567 mph (912 km/h) at 32,810 ft (10 000 m) or Mach 0·84; tactical radius (training mission LO-LO-LO profile), 267 mls (430 km); ferry range (max. internal fuel), 1,243 mls (2 000 km), (with two 68 Imp gal/310 J external tanks), 1,678 mls (2 700 km); max. climb, 11,220 ft/min (57 m/sec); ceiling, 45,000 ft (13 715 m).
Weights: Empty, 7,716 lb (3 500 kg); normal loaded (clean), 11,023 lb (5 000 kg); normal take-off (close air support), 13,448 lb (6 100 kg); max. overload, 15,983 lb (7 250 kg).
Armament: External centreline gun pod with (Alpha Jet E) 30-mm DEFA 533 or (Alpha Jet A) 27-mm Mauser cannon. Two 1,500-lb (680-kg) and two 750-lb (340-kg) capacity wing stores stations with max. load of 4,850 lb (2 200 kg).
Status: First of four prototypes flown October 26, 1973, with first production Alpha Jet E flying on November 4, 1977, and first production Alpha Jet A on April 12, 1978. Production rate of six monthly in both France and Germany at beginning of 1980 when 110 had been delivered against orders for 144 for France, 175 for Germany, 33 for Belgium, 12 for Ivory Coast, 24 for Morocco, 12 for Nigeria and five for Togo. Total of 230 is scheduled to be delivered by end of 1980.
Notes: Two final assembly lines (Toulouse and Munich).

DASSAULT-BREGUET/DORNIER ALPHA JET

Dimensions: Span, 29 ft 11 in (9,11 m); length, 40 ft 3 in (12,29 m); height, 13 ft 9 in (4,19 m); wing area, 188 sq ft (15,50 m²).

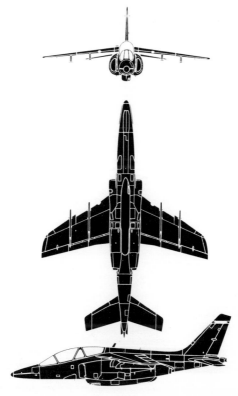

DE HAVILLAND CANADA DASH 7

County of Origin: Canada.

Type: STOL short-haul commercial transport.

Power-Plant: Four 1,120 shp Pratt & Whitney (Canada) PT6A-50 turboprops.

Performance: Max. cruise, 269 mph (434 km/h) at 15,000 ft (4 570 m); long-range cruise, 235 mph (379 km/h) at 20,000 ft (6 560 m); range (with 12,150-lb/5 511-kg payload), 696 mls (1 120 km); max. range, 1,807 mls (2 910 km).

Weights: Empty equipped, 26, 850 lb (12 179 kg); max. take-off, 43,500 lb (19 731 kg).

Accommodation: Flight crew of two and standard seating arrangement for 50 passengers in pairs on each side of central aisle with 300 cu ft (8,49 m³) baggage compartment or 240 cu ft (6,80 m³) compartment and buffet. Various optional passenger/cargo arrangements (e.g., 34 passengers and one pallet, 26 passengers and two pallets or 18 passengers and three pallets.)

Status: Two pre-production aircraft flown on March 27 and June 26, 1975. Production commitment for 50 aircraft, of which first flown April 1977, and first customer delivery (second production aircraft to Rocky Mountain) October 1977. Orders totalled 67 at the beginning of 1980, when production rate was 2–3 monthly with some 25 delivered.

Notes: Current orders include two Dash 7s for the Canadian Armed Forces for operation in Europe (one of which is illustrated above) and two examples of a maritime surveillance version, the Dash 7R Ranger, for the Canadian Coast Guard. The Ranger will be delivered in 1980 and will offer extended payload and range performance, and increased fuel capacity.

DE HAVILLAND CANADA DASH 7

Dimensions: Span, 93 ft 0 in (28,35 m); length, 80 ft 7¾ in (24,58 m); height, 26 ft 2 in (7,98 m); wing area, 860 sq ft (79,90 m²).

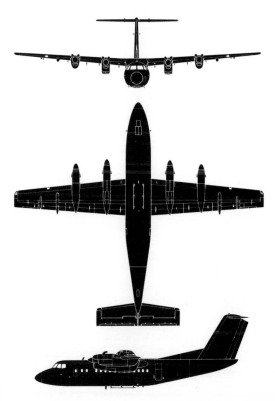

EMBRAER BMB-121 XINGU

Country of Origin: Brazil.

Type: Light business executive transport.

Power Plant: Two 680 shp Pratt & Whitney PT6A-28 turboprops.

Performance: Max. cruise, 280 mph (450 km/h) at 11,000 ft (3 353 m); initial climb, 1,400 ft/min (7,11 m/sec); service ceiling, 26,000 ft (7 925 m); range (with 1,985-lb/900-kg payload), 1,036 mls (1 668 km) at 20,000 ft (6 100 m); max. range (with 1,344-lb/610-kg payload), 1,462 mls (2 353 km).

Weights: Empty equipped, 7,716 lb (3 500 kg); max. take-off, 12,500 lb (5 670 kg).

Accommodation: Two seats side-by-side on flight deck and individual seats for five—six passengers in main cabin. Alternative high-density configuration for nine passengers three abreast in main cabin.

Status: Prototype flown October 10, 1976, with first production aircraft flown on May 20, 1977. First customer delivery June 1978, and 48 scheduled to be delivered by September 1981, when production will switch to Xingu 2.

Notes: The Xingu has undergone a number of changes since it initially appeared in production form (see 1978 edition), having acquired redesigned vertical tail surfaces, a ventral fin, extended wingtips to permit larger ailerons, and other changes. Six have been supplied to the Brazilian Air Force as VU-9s, and a stretched variant, the Xingu 2, with a 33-in (84-cm) increase in fuselage length permitting a normal passenger capacity of eight and PT6A-42 engines is scheduled to commence flight testing in the first half of 1980. The Xingu is evolved from the EMB 110 Bandeirante (see 1979 edition).

94

EMBRAER EMB-121 XINGU

Dimensions: Span, 47 ft 5 in (14,45 m); length, 40 ft 2¼ in (12,25 m); height, 15 ft 6½ in (4,74 m); wing area, 296 sq ft (27,50 m²).

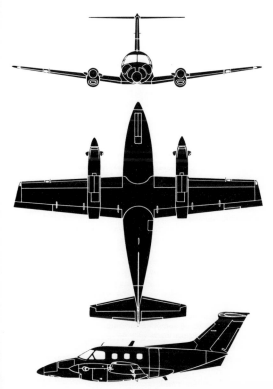

EMBRAER EMB-312

Country of Origin: Brazil.

Type: Tandem two-seat basic-advanced trainer.

Power Plant: One 750 shp Pratt & Whitney PT6A-25C turboprop.

Performance: (Estimated at 5,180 lb/2 350 kg) Max. speed, 284 mph (457 km/h) at 13,120 ft (4 000 m); max. continuous cruise, 276 mph (444 km/h); initial climb, 2,130 ft/min (10,8 m/sec); service ceiling (at 4,640 lb/2 100 kg), 32,600 ft (9 935 m); range (with 30 min reserves) at long-range cruise at 15,000 ft (4 575 m), 1,312 mls (2 112 km).

Weights: Max. take-off, 5,180 lb (2 350 kg).

Armament: (For weapons training) Two 0·5-in (12,7-mm) machine gun pods each with 350 rounds, four 250-lb (113,4-kg) bombs, or four rocket pods.

Status: The first of two flying prototypes scheduled to commence its test programme September–October 1980, with production deliveries to commence late 1982 or early 1983.

Notes: The EMB-312 has been designed to meet the requirements of a Brazilian Air Force specification, the service having a requirement for 150 aircraft in this category, the Air Force designation being T-27. The EMB-312 will cater for operations from semi-prepared airstrips and although intended primarily as a pilot trainer, four 330-lb (150-kg) capacity wing hardpoints are being provided for bombs, gun or rocket pods, and studies are being made of internal gun armament to suit the aircraft for the counter-insurgency role. The EMB-312 utilises the most modern constructional techniques, making extensive use of integral machining, chemical milling and metal-to-metal bonding.

EMBRAER EMB-312

Dimensions: Span, 36 ft 4½ in (11,09 m); length, 33 ft 3½ in (10,15 m); height, 11 ft 1⅞ in (3,40 m); wing area, 204·52 sq ft (19,00 m²).

FAIRCHILD (NIGHT/ADVERSE WEATHER)
A-10 THUNDERBOLT II

Country of Origin: USA.

Type: Two-seat night and adverse weather close support aircraft.

Power Plant: Two 9,065 lb (4 112 kg) General Electric TF34-GE-100 turbofans.

Performance: Never-exceed speed, 460 mph (740 km/h); max. speed (clean), 432 mph (695 km/h) at sea level; max. combat speed (with six AGM-65A Maverick missiles), 420 mph (676 km/h) at 5,000 ft (1 525 m); max. continuous cruise, 382 mph (615 km/h); operational radius for close air support mission (with 2 hr loiter), 280 mls (450 km), reconnaissance mission, 450 mls (724 km).

Weights: Basic equipped, 25,830 lb (11 716 kg); max. take-off, 44,162 lb (20 032 kg).

Armament: One seven-barrel 30-mm GAU-8A Avenger rotary cannon. Eleven external stations for maximum of 9,540 lb of ordnance.

Status: The prototype night and adverse weather A-10 flew on May 4, 1979, and has 94 per cent structural and 82 per cent equipment commonality with the current production single-seat A-10A, the first of two prototypes of which flew on May 10, 1972. Approximately 290 A-10As delivered by beginning of 1980 (against planned USAF procurement of 739) when production rate was 12 monthly.

Notes: An enhanced capability two-seat development of the single-seat clear-weather A-10A (see 1979 edition), the night and adverse weather version of the Thunderbolt II has multimode terrain-following radar, forward-looking infrared and laser rangefinding.

FAIRCHILD (NIGHT/ADVERSE WEATHER)
A-10 THUNDERBOLT II

Dimensions: Span, 57 ft 6 in (17,53 m); length, 53 ft 4 in (16,25 m); height, 16 ft 4 in (4,98 m); wing area, 506 sq ft (47,01 m²).

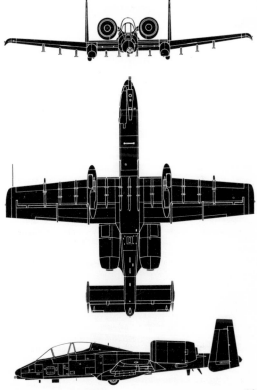

FOKKER F27MPA MARITIME

Country of Origin: Netherlands.

Type: Medium-range maritime patrol and surveillance aircraft.

Power Plant: Two 2,250 eshp Rolls-Royce Dart 536-7R turboprops.

Performance: Cruising speed (at 40,000 lb/18 145 kg), 265 mph (427 km/h) at 20,000 ft (6 095 m); typical search speed, 168 mph (270 km/h) at 2,000 ft (610 m); service ceiling (at 45,000 lb/20 412 kg), 23,000 ft (7 010 m); max. range (cruising at 20,000 ft/6 095 m with 30 min loiter and 5% reserves, with pylon tanks), 2,548 mls (4 100 km); max. endurance, 11 hrs.

Weights: Typical zero fuel, 28,097 lb (12 745 kg); max. take-off, 44,996 lb (20 410 kg).

Accommodation: Standard accommodation for crew of six comprising pilot, co-pilot, navigator, radar operator and two observers.

Status: Prototype F27 Maritime (converted F27 Mk 100 No. 68) flown on March 25, 1976, and first production aircraft was delivered in the summer of 1977. Initial customers were the Peruvian Navy (2) and the Spanish search and rescue service (3).

Notes: Derivative of Mk 400 transport with Litton AN/APS-503F search radar, Litton LTN-72 long-range inertial navigation system, blister windows adjacent to marine marker launcher and provision for pylon fuel tanks. The Maritime is ostensibly a civil patrol aircraft for off-shore "sovereignty" operations, such as oil-rig and fisheries protection, but has several potential military customers, being suitable for maritime reconnaissance. F27 orders (all versions) totalled 490 (excluding 205 built by Fairchild) at the beginning of 1980.

FOKKER F27MPA MARITIME

Dimensions: Span, 95 ft 1$\frac{4}{5}$ in (29,00 m); length, 77 ft 3$\frac{1}{2}$ in (23,56 m); height, 28 ft 6$\frac{7}{10}$ in; wing area, 753·47 sq ft (70.00 m²).

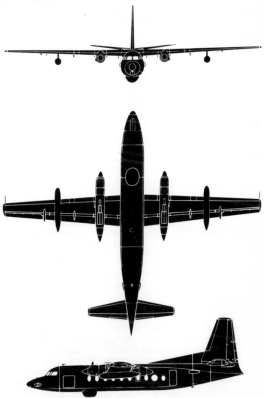

FOKKER F28 FELLOWSHIP MK. 4000

Country of Origin: Netherlands.

Type: Short-haul commercial transport.

Power Plant: Two 9,850 lb (4 468 kg) Rolls-Royce RB.183-2 Spey Mk 555-15H turbofans.

Performance: Max cruise, 523 mph (843 km/h) at 23,000 ft (7 000 m); econ. cruise. 487 mph (783 km/h) at 32,000 ft (9 755 m); range cruise, 421 mph (678 km/h) at 30,000 ft (9 145 m); range (with max. payload), 1,160 mls (1 870 km) at econ. cruise, (with max. fuel), 2,566 mls (4 130 km); max. cruise altitude, 35,000 ft (10 675 m).

Weights: Operational empty (typical), 37,736 lb (17 117 kg); max. take-off, 71,000 lb (32 200 kg).

Accommodation: Flight crew of two and typical single-class configuration for 85 passengers five abreast.

Status: First and second F28 prototypes flown May 9 and August 3, 1967, first delivery following on February 24, 1969. A total of 151 F28s (all versions) ordered by 1980.

Notes: The F28 Mks. 1000 and 2000 are now out of production (after completion of 97 and 10 respectively), having been replaced by the Mks. 3000 and 4000, both having unslatted, longer-span wings and Spey Mk. 555–15H engines. The former has the 80 ft 6½ in (24,55 m) fuselage of the Mk. 1000 and the latter has the longer fuselage of the Mk. 2000. Also on offer is the slatted Mk. 6000 (see 1977 edition) with the same high-density accommodation as the Mk. 4000 and having improved field performance and payload/range capabilities.

A version that was proposed during 1978 was the Mk. 6600 which was a stretched version of the Mk. 6000 with 87 in (220 cm) inserted in the fuselage and Mk. 555-15K engines, and at the beginning of 1980, studies were continuing of the 132-seat-plus development follow-on to the F28, the F29.

FOKKER F28 FELLOWSHIP MK. 4000

Dimensions: Span, 82 ft 3 in (25,07 m); length 97 ft 1¾ in (29,61 m); height, 27 ft 9½ in (8,47 m); wing area, 850 sq ft (78,97 m²).

GAF NOMAD SEARCHMASTER

Country of Origin: Australia.

Type: Light maritime patrol and surveillance aircraft.

Power Plant: Two 400 shp Allison 250-B17B turboprops.

Performance: (Searchmaster B at 8,500 lb/3 855 kg) Max. cruising speed, 195 mph (313 km/h) at 5,000 ft (1 525 m); cruise (75% max. cruise rating), 176 mph (282 km/h); range (with 45 min reserve), 920 mls (1 482 km) at 10,000 ft (3 050 m); typical mission, 8 hr search at 161 mph (259 km/h) at 5,000 ft (1 525 m); initial climb, 1,460 ft/min (7,4 m/sec); service ceiling (at 8,000 lb/3 629 kg), 23,500 ft (7 165 m).

Weights: Operational empty (less equipment options), 4,783 lb (2 170 kg); max. take-off, 8,500 lb (3 855 kg).

Accommodation: Basic crew of four—five, comprising one or two pilots, a tactical navigator and one or two observer/despatchers.

Status: The Searchmaster is a derivative of the Nomad N22B light utility transport, the initial version, the Searchmaster B, being introduced in 1975, and the Searchmaster L commencing its test programme in 1978. Approximately 90 Nomads (all versions) had been completed by the beginning of 1980, when production was running at two monthly.

Notes: The Searchmaster B (described and illustrated above) and Searchmaster L (illustrated opposite) differ primarily in equipment fit, the former having a forward-looking Bendix RDR 1400 radar with 18-in (45,72-cm) scanner and the latter having Litton LASR 2 with a 36-in (91,44-cm) 360-deg scanner.

104

GAF NOMAD SEARCHMASTER

Dimensions: Span, 54 ft 0 in (16,46 m); length, 41 ft 2½ in (12,57 m); height, 18 ft 1½ in (5,52 m); wing area, 324 sq ft (30,10 m²).

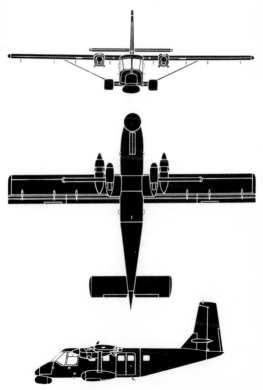

GATES LEARJET 36A SEA PATROL

Country of Origin: USA.

Type: Light coastal patrol and maritime surveillance aircraft.

Power Plant' Two 3,500 lb (1 588 kg) Garrett AiResearch TFE 731-2 turbofans.

Performance: High-altitude cruise, 469 mph (755 km/h) at 37,000–41,000 ft (11 280–12 495 m); medium-altitude cruise, 372 mph (599 km/h) at 15,000–25,000 ft (4 570–7 620 m); low-altitude cruise, 296 mph (476 km/h) at sea level to 2,000 ft (610 m); initial climb, 4,525 ft/min (22,98 m/sec); range, 2,880 mls (4 635 km) at high altitude, 2,085 mls (3 355 km) at medium altitude, 1,345 mls (2 165 km) at low altitude.

Weights: Max. take-off, 18,000 lb (8 164 kg).

Accommodation: Flight crew of two with dual controls and provision in main cabin for radar operator and two observers.

Status: Prototype Sea Patrol model (based on Learjet 35A) flown spring 1979, with deliveries (based on either Model 35A or Model 36A) offered for 1980.

Notes: Sea Patrol version of Learjet 35A/36A (see 1977 edition) has 360 deg surveillance radar, forward-looking infrared sensors, low-light-level television and an ejector rack beneath each wing for stores (e.g. rescue pods, sono-buoys, flares, smoke markers) weighing up to 500 lb (227 kg). By comparison with the 35A, the 36A has increased fuel capacity. The Sea Patrol model is suitable for the location and detection of surface vessels, the identification of targets and determination of target activities.

GATES LEARJET 36A SEA PATROL

Dimensions: Span, 39 ft 8 in (12,09 m); length, 48 ft 8 in
(14,33 m); height, 12 ft 3 in (3,73 m); wing area, 253·3 sq ft
(23,5 m²).

GATES LEARJET LONGHORN 55

Country of Origin: USA.
Type: Light business executive transport.
Power Plant: Two 3,650 lb (1 657 kg) Garrett AiResearch TFE 731–3–100B turbofans.
Performance: Max. speed, 534 mph (860 km/h) above 24,000 ft (7 315 m); initial climb, 5,020 ft./min (25,5 m/sec); initial cruise altitude, 44,200 ft (13 470 m); max. ceiling, 51,000 ft (15 545 m); max. range (with four passengers), 3,000 mls (4 828 km), (no payload), 3,252 mls (5 232 km).
Weights: Empty equipped, 10,508 lb (4 766 kg); max. take-off, 19,000 lb (8 618 kg).
Accommodation: Flight crew of two and up to nine passengers in main cabin.
Status: First prototype Longhorn 50 series (Longhorn 55) flown April 19, 1979, with second prototype following on November 15, 1979. First customer deliveries scheduled for June 1980, with an initial production rate of one aircraft per month rising to four per month by January 1981.
Notes: Combining the wing development for the Longhorn 28/29 (see 1979 edition) with an entirely new fuselage, the Longhorn 50 series comprises three models, all possessing the same external dimensions but differing in cabin lengths and fuel capacities, with the Longhorn 56 having a higher take-off weight of 20,500 lb (9 299 kg). By comparison with the Longhorn 55 described above, the Longhorn 54 has a maximum range of 2,503 mls (4 028 km) and the Longhorn 56 has a maximum range of 3,580 mls (5 760 km) with four passengers in both cases. Deliveries of Learjets of all types were approaching 1,000 aircraft by early 1980, when production was concentrating on the Learjet 30 series (i.e., the 35A and 36A) and the Longhorn 50 series (i.e., 54, 55 and 56).

GATES LEARJET LONGHORN 55

Dimensions: Span, 43 ft 9½ in (13,34 m); length, 55 ft 1½ in (16,79 m); height, 14 ft 8 in (4,47 m); wing area, 264·5 sq ft (24,57 m²).

GENERAL DYNAMICS F-16

Country of Origin: USA.
Type: Single-seat air combat fighter (F-16A) and two-seat operational trainer (F-16B).
Power Plant: One (approx.) 25,000 lb (11 340 kg) reheat Pratt & Whitney F100-PW-100(3) turbofan.
Performance: Max. speed (with two Sidewinder AAMs), 1,255 mph (2 020 km/h) at 36,000 ft (10 970 m), or Mach 1·95, 915 mph (1 472 km/h) at sea level, or Mach 1·2; tactical radius (interdiction mission HI-LO-HI on internal fuel with six Mk. 82 bombs), 340 mls (550 km); ferry range, 2,300+ mls (3 700+ km); initial climb, 62,000 ft/min (315 m/sec); service ceiling, 52,000 ft (15 850 m).
Weights: Operational empty, 14,567 lb (6 613 kg); loaded (intercept mission with two Sidewinders), 22,785 lb (10 344 kg); max. take-off, 33,000 lb (14 969 kg).
Armament: One 20-mm M61A-1 Vulcan multi-barrel cannon with 515 rounds and max. external ordnance load of 15,200 lb (6 894 kg) with reduced internal fuel or 11,000 lb (4 990 kg) with full internal fuel distributed between nine stations (two wingtip, six underwing and one fuselage).
Status: First of two (YF-16) prototypes flown on January 20, 1974. First of eight pre-production aircraft (six single-seat F-16As and two two-seat F-16Bs) flown December 8, 1976, and first two-seater (fourth aircraft) on August 8, 1977, with the first full production F-16A flying on August 7, 1978. Current planning calls for 1,388 F-16s for USAF (including 204 F-16Bs), and 75 for Israel. Licence manufacture by European consortium for Netherlands (84 plus 18 on option), Belgium (102 plus 14 on option), Denmark (48 plus 10 on option) and Norway (72). A two-seat F-16B is illustrated above.

110

GENERAL DYNAMICS F-16

Dimensions: Span (excluding missiles), 31 ft 0 in (9,45 m);
length, 47 ft 7¾ in (14,52 m); height, 16 ft 5¼ in (5,01 m);
wing area, 300 sq ft (27,87 m²).

GRUMMAN E-2C HAWKEYE

Country of Origin: USA.

Type: Shipboard airborne early warning, surface surveillance and strike control aircraft.

Power Plant: Two 4,910 ehp Allison T56-A-425 turboprops.

Performance: Max. speed (at max. take-off), 348 mph (560 km/h) at 10,000 ft (3 050 m); max. range cruise, 309 mph (498 km/h); max. endurance, 6·1 hrs; mission endurance (at 230 mls/370 km from base), 4·0 hrs; ferry range, 1,604 mls (2 580 km); initial climb, 2,515 ft/min (12,8 m/sec); service ceiling, 30,800 ft (9 390 m).

Weights: Empty, 38,009 lb (17 240 kg); max. take-off, 51,900 lb (23 540 kg).

Accommodation: Crew of five comprising flight crew of two and Airborne Tactical Data System team of three, each at an independent operating station.

Status: First of two E-2C prototypes flown on January 20, 1971, with first production aircraft flying on September 23, 1972. Fifty-two E-2Cs delivered by beginning of Fiscal Year 1980 against total US Navy requirement for 77 plus four for Israel (one of which is illustrated above) and four ordered by Japan in September 1979 for delivery 1982–83, with a follow-on order for a further four anticipated.

Notes: Current production model of Hawkeye following 59 E-2As (all subsequently updated to E-2B standard) and, since December 1976, equipped with advanced APS-125 radar processing system. This system is able to operate independently, in co-operation with other aircraft, or in concert with ground environments. A training version currently serving with the US Navy is designated TE-2C, and production of the E-2C Hawkeye is scheduled to continue through 1984.

GRUMMAN E-2C HAWKEYE

Dimensions: Span, 80 ft 7 in (24,56 m); length, 57 ft 7 in
(17,55 m); height, 18 ft 4 in (5,59 m); wing area, 700 sq ft
(65,03 m²).

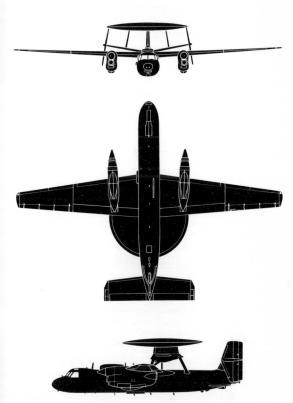

GRUMMAN F-14A TOMCAT

Country of Origin: USA.

Type: Two-seat shipboard multi-purpose fighter.

Power Plant: Two 20,900 lb (9 480 kg) reheat Pratt & Whitney TF30-P-412A turbofans.

Performance: Design max. speed (clean), 1,545 mph (2 486 km/h) at 40,000 ft (12 190 m) or Mach 2·34; max. speed (internal fuel and four AIM-7 missiles at 55,000 lb/24 948 kg), 910 mph (1 470 km/h) at sea level or Mach 1·2; tactical radius (internal fuel and four AIM-7 missiles plus allowance for 2 min combat at 10,000 ft/3 050 m), approx. 450 mls (725 km); time to 60,000 ft (18 290 m) at 55,000 lb (24 948 kg), 2·1 min.

Weights: Empty equipped, 40,070 lb (18 176 kg); normal take-off (internal fuel and four AIM-7 AAMs), 55,000 lb (24 948 kg); max. take-off (ground attack/interdiction), 68,567 lb (31 101 kg).

Armament: One 20-mm M-61A1 rotary cannon and (intercept mission) six AIM-7E/F Sparrow and four AIM-9G/H Sidewinder AAMs or six AIM-54A and two AIM-9G/H AAMs.

Status: First of 12 research and development aircraft flown December 21, 1970, and US Navy plans to acquire a total of 521 aircraft (proposing in 1979 to increase this total to 601 to meet its 18-squadron target), but changes in defence planning call for the termination of F-14 production in Fiscal 1982 at a total of 467 US Navy aircraft. Production of the F-14A totalled some 500 at the beginning of 1980, with production running at two monthly. Seventy-seven (of 80) F-14As supplied to Iran awaiting disposal at beginning of 1980.

GRUMMAN F-14A TOMCAT

Dimensions: Span (max.), 64 ft $1\frac{1}{2}$ in (19,55 m), (min.), 37 ft 7 in (11,45 m), (overswept on deck), 33 ft $3\frac{1}{2}$ in (10,15 m); length, 61 ft $11\frac{7}{8}$ in (18,90 m); height, 16 ft 0 in (4,88 m); wing area, 565 sq ft (52,5 m²).

GULFSTREAM AMERICAN GULFSTREAM I-C

Country of Origin: USA.

Type: Third-level commuter transport.

Power Plant: Two 2,210 eshp Rolls-Royce Dart 529 turboprops.

Performance: (Estimated) Max. cruise, 345 mph (555 km/h) at 25,000 ft (7 620 m); range (at max. cruise with reserves for 173 mls/278 km and 45 min hold), 715 mls (1 150 km) with 38 passengers, 440 mls (708 km) with 8,500 lb (3 856 kg) cargo; ferry range, 2,130 mls (3 428 km); max. altitude, 30,000 ft (9 145 m).

Weights: Basic operational (passenger version), 23,550 lb (10 682 kg); max. take-off, 36,000 lb (16 325 kg).

Accommodation: Flight crew of two and optional arrangements in main cabin for 32 or 38 passengers in three-abreast seating. Optional freight door in rear fuselage side.

Status: Prototype (converted from standard Gulfstream I airframe) was flown for the first time on October 25, 1979. Initial customer deliveries scheduled for second half of 1981.

Notes: The Gulfstream I-C is a new-production stretched derivative of the Gulfstream I executive transport, manufacture of which ended in 1958. The prototype, illustrated above, retains the oval cabin windows of the Gulfstream executive transport, but the planned production Gulfstream I-C (illustrated by the drawing opposite) has rectangular cabin windows and a reshaped nose. Optional all-freight and mixed passenger/freight versions with large rear cargo door are on offer, and proposals exist for the conversion of existing Gulfstream Is (200 built) to I-C standard.

116

GULFSTREAM AMERICAN GULFSTREAM I-C

Dimensions: Span, 78 ft 4 in (23,87 m); length, 74 ft 3 in (22,63 m); height, 22 ft 11 in (6,98 m); wing area, 610 sq ft (56,67 m²).

GULFSTREAM AMERICAN
GULFSTREAM III

Country of Origin: USA.

Type: Light business executive transport.

Power Plant: Two 11,400 lb (5176 kg) Rolls-Royce RB.163-25 Spey Mk. 511-8 turbofans.

Performance: (Estimated) Max. cruising speed, 560 mph (900 km/h) at 45,000 ft (13 715 m) or Mach 0·85; long-range cruise, 511 mph (822 km/h) or Mach 0·775; max. range (with 1,600-lb/726-kg payload and 30 min reserve), 4,660 mls (7 490 km).

Weights: Typical operational empty, 37,720 lb (17 125 kg); max. take-off, 65,500 lb (29 737 kg).

Accommodation: Crew of two or three and various layouts for up to 19 passengers in main cabin.

Status: Gulfstream III prototype was first flown on December 2, 1979, with the first customer delivery scheduled for spring 1980, in which year 18 will be built, production tempo rising thereafter to two monthly in 1982.

Notes: The Gulfstream III is a progressive development of the (formerly Grumman) Gulfstream II (see 1969 edition) which has been in continuous production since 1965, with the 258th and last being delivered in December 1979 when the earlier model was superseded by the Gulfstream III on the assembly line. The new variant has a lengthened fuselage by comparison with the Gulfstream II, a modified wing structure with NASA-style winglets, an extended nose radome, a wrap-around windscreen and improved crew accommodation. Gulfstream III wings are to be made available for retrofit to existing Gulfstream IIs from early 1981, the new wing affording improved range and field performance.

GULFSTREAM AMERICAN GULFSTREAM III

Dimensions: Span, 77 ft 10 in (23,72 m); length 82 ft 11 in (25,27 m); height, 23 ft 8 in (7,21 m); wing area, 934·6 sq ft (86,82 m²).

GULFSTREAM AMERICAN HUSTLER 500

Country of Origin: USA.

Type: Light business executive transport.

Power Plant: One 900 shp Garrett AiResearch TPE 331–10–501 turboprop and one 2,200 lb (998 kg) Pratt & Whitney JT15D-1 turbofan.

Performance: (Estimated) Max. cruise, 461 mph (741 km/h) at 25,000 ft (7 620 m), TPE 331 only), 300 mph (483 km/h) at 13,000 ft (3 960 m), (JT15D-1 only), 340 mph (547 km/h) at 20,000 ft (6 095 m); initial climb, 3,450 ft/min (17,5 m/sec); range at max. cruise (45 min reserves), 1,290 mls (2 076 km) at 25,000 ft (7 620 m), 2,300 mls (3 700 km) at 403 mph (648 km/h) at 38,000 ft (11 580 m), (with JT15D-1 shut down after 1·2 hrs), 2,764 mls (4 447 km) at 30,000 ft (9 145 m).

Weights: Empty, 5,430 lb (2 463 kg); max. take-off, 10,000 lb (4 536 kg).

Accommodation: Pilot and co-pilot/passenger side-by-side on flight deck and up to seven passengers in main cabin.

Status: Prototype Hustler 500 was scheduled to fly late 1979, with two further test and development aircraft following during the first half of 1980, and initial customer deliveries early 1981.

Notes: The Hustler 500 is a progressive development of the Hustler 400 prototype, which first flown on January 11, 1978, was powered solely by an 850 shp Pratt & Whitney PT6A-41 turboprop. This engine is replaced in the Hustler 500 by the TPE 331 owing to the aerodynamic and performance advantages offered by the single exhaust of the Garrett unit.

GULFSTREAM AMERICAN HUSTLER 500

Dimensions: Span, 34 ft 5 in (10,49 m); length, 41 ft 3 in (12,57 m); height, 13 ft 2½ in (4,02 m); wing area, 192·76 sq ft (17,90 m²).

(HARBIN) YUONG-SHUCHI 11 (Y-11)

Country of Origin: Chinese Republic.

Type: Light utility transport.

Power Plant: Two 285 hp Jia Hou-sai 6itsi (AI-14R) nine-cylinder radial air-cooled engines.

Performance: Max. speed, 137 mph (220 km/h); cruise (at 57% power), 102 mph (165 km/h); service ceiling, 13,120 ft (4 000 m); range, 618 mls (995 km); max. endurance, 7·5 hrs.

Weights: Empty, 4,520 lb (2 050 kg); max. take-off, 7,715 lb (3 500 kg).

Accommodation: Side-by-side seats on flight deck for pilot and co-pilot/passenger and various arrangements for six—eight passengers in main cabin, or (aeromedicl role) four stretcher patients and one medical attendant.

Status: Prototypes of the Y-11 were completed and flown at the State Aircraft Factory at Shenyang in 1975, series production being initiated by the State Aircraft Factory at Harbin in 1977.

Notes: The Y-11 (Type 11 Transport Plane, or *Yuong-shuchi Sinshi-shi*) is intended as a successor to the licence-manufactured Antonov An-2 (Y-5) and is a multi-role STOL aeroplane for rough-field operation and having both take-off and landing rolls of 153 yards (140 m). The Y-11 is employed in the agricultural role with four insecticide atomisers under the wings and two more under the stub wings, a hopper inserted in the fuselage accommodating 1,885 lb (855 kg) of powder or 214 Imp gal (973 l) of liquid.

(HARBIN) YUONG-SHUCHI 11 (Y-11)

Dimensions: Span, 55 ft 9¼ in (17,00 m): length, 39 ft 4½ in (12,00 m); height, 15 ft 2¾ in (4,64 m); wing area, 366 sq ft (34,00 m²).

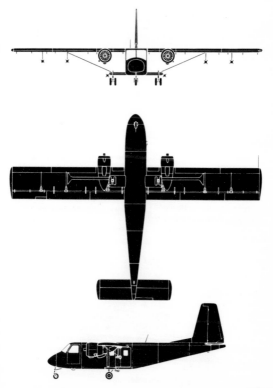

IAI KFIR-C2

Country of Origin: Israel.

Type: Single-seat multi-role fighter.

Power Plant: One 11,870 lb (5 385 kg) dry and 17,900 lb (8 120 kg) Bet-Shemesh-built General Electric J79-GE-17 turbojet.

Performance: (Estimated) Max. speed (50% fuel and two Shafrir AAMs), 850 mph (1 368 km/h) at 1,000 ft (305 m) or Mach 1·12, 1,420 mph (2 285 km/h) above 36,000 ft (10 970 m) or Mach 2·3; max. low-level climb rate, 47,250 ft/min (240 m/sec); max. ceiling, 59,050 ft (18 000 m); radius of action (air superiority mission with two 110 Imp gal/500 l drop tanks), 323 mls (520 km), (ground attack mission hi-lo-hi profile), 745 mls (1 200 km).

Weights: Loaded (intercept with 50% fuel and two AAMs), 20,700 lb (9 390 kg); max. take-off, 32,190 lb (14 600 kg).

Armament: Two 30-mm DEFA cannon with 125 rpg and (intercept) two or four Rafael Shafrir AAMs, or (ground attack) up to 8,820 lb (4 000 kg) of external ordnance.

Status: Initial production version of Kfir delivered to Israeli air arm from April 1975 with deliveries of improved Kfir-C2 having commenced early in 1977, production rate at the beginning of **1980** reportedly being 2·5 aircraft monthly.

Notes: The Kfir-C2 differs from the initial production Kfir (Young Lion) in having modifications designed primarily to improve combat manœuvrability, these comprising canard auxiliary surfaces which result in a close-coupled canard configuration, dog-tooth wing leading-edge extensions and nose strakes. Equipped with a dual-mode ranging radar, the Kfir is based on the Mirage 5 airframe.

IAI KFIR-C2

Dimensions: Span, 26 ft 11½ in (8,22 m); length, 51 ft 0¼ in (15,55 m); height, 13 ft 11½ in (4,25 m); wing area (excluding canard and dogtooth), 375·12 sq ft (34,85 m²).

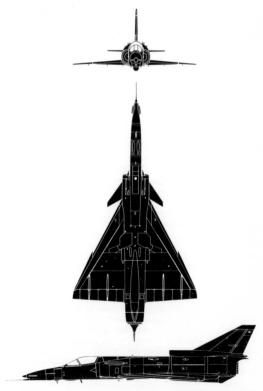

IAI WESTWIND 2

Country of Origin: Israel.

Type: Light business executive transport.

Power Plant: Two 3,700 lb (1 678 kg) Garrett AiResearch TFE 731-3-1G turbofans.

Performance: Max. speed, 542 mph (872 km/h) at sea level to 19,400 ft (5 900 m); max. operating speed, 414 mph (666 km/h) at sea level to 19,400 ft; econ. cruise, 460 mph (741 km/h) at 41,000 ft (12 500 m); max. initial climb, 5,000 ft/min (25,4 m/sec); max range (with four passengers and reserves), 3,340 mls (5 375 km).

Weights: Empty equipped, 12,830 lb (5 819 kg); max. take-off, 23,500 lb (10 660 kg).

Accommodation: Two seats side-by-side on flight deck with various arrangements in main cabin for 7–10 passengers.

Status: The Westwind 2 was first flown in April 1979 and customer deliveries are scheduled for second half of 1980. The Westwind 2 is being produced in parallel with the Westwind 1, combined production rate of which was scheduled to attain four monthly in January 1980, at which time orders for turbo-fan-powered IAI 1124 series Westwinds exceeded 100 aircraft with approximately 90 delivered by the beginning of 1980.

Notes: The Westwind 2 is a longer-range development of the Westwind 1 with a higher-efficiency aerofoil and winglets combined with the wingtip tanks. The Westwind 1, which succeeded the Westwind 1124 (the first of the Westwind series with TFE 731 turbofans), introduced increased fuel capacity and improved accommodation.

126

IAI WESTWIND 2

Dimensions: Span, 44 ft 9½ in (13,65 m); length, 52 ft 3 in (15,93 m); height, 15 ft 9½ in (4,81 m); wing area, 308·26 sq ft (28,64 m²).

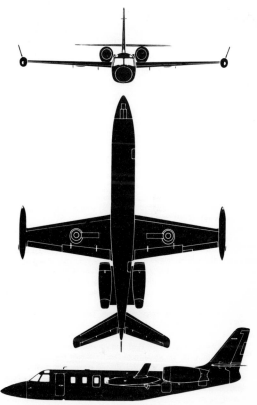

ILYUSHIN IL-76T (CANDID)

Country of Origin: USSR.

Type: Heavy commercial and military freighter.

Power Plant: Four 26,455 lb (12 000 kg) Soloviev D-30KP turbofans.

Performance: Max. cruise, 497 mph (800 km/h) at 29,530 ft (9 000 m); range cruise, 466 mph (750 km/h) at 39,370 ft (12 000 m); max. range (with reserves), 4,163 mls (6 700 km); range with max. payload (88,185 lb/40 000 kg), 3,107 mls (5 000 km).

Weights: Max. take-off, 374,790 lb (170 000 kg).

Accommodation: Normal flight crew of four with navigator below flight deck in glazed nose. Pressurised hold for containerised and other freight, wheeled and tracked vehicles, etc. Military version has pressurised tail station for sighting 23-mm cannon barbette.

Status: First of four prototypes flown on March 25, 1971, with production deliveries to Soviet Air Force commencing 1974, and to Aeroflot (Il-76T) 1976. Export deliveries began in 1978 to the Iraqi Air Force and Iraq Airways.

Notes: The Il-76 is being manufactured in both commercial and military versions, the former (Il-76T) being illustrated above and the latter on opposite page. The current production Il-76 has some 20% more fuel capacity than the initial version and a 1,056-mile (1 700-km) range increase, max. take-off weight having been increased by 28,660 lb (13 000 kg). A flight refuelling tanker version of the Il-76 has been developed for the Soviet Air Force, and the aircraft possesses outstanding short-field capability and may be operated from unprepared airstrips, having a multi-wheel undercarriage with variable-pressure tyres.

ILYUSHIN IL-76T (CANDID)

Dimensions: Span, 165 ft 8⅓ in (50,50 m); length, 152 ft 10¼ in (46,59 m); height, 48 ft 5⅛ in (14,76 m); wing area, 3,229·2 sq ft (300,00 m²).

ILYUSHIN IL-86 (CAMBER)

Country of Origin: USSR.
Type: Medium-haul commercial transport.
Power Plant: Four 28,660 lb (13 000 kg) Kuznetsov NK-86 turbofans.
Performance: Max. cruise, 590 mph (950 km/h) at 29,530 ft (9 000 m); long-range cruise, 559 mph (900 km/h) at 36,090 ft (11 000 m); range (with max. playload—350 passengers), 2,485 mls (4 000 km), (with 250 passengers), 3,107 mls (5 000 km).
Weights: Max. take-off, 454,150 lb (206 000 kg).
Accommodation: Standard flight crew of three—four and up to 350 passengers in basic nine-abreast seating with two aisles (divided between three cabins accommodating 111, 141 and 98 passengers respectively).
Status: First prototype flown on December 22, 1976, and production prototype flown on October 24, 1977. Service entry (with Aeroflot) is scheduled for 1980, and production is a collaborative effort with Polish WSK-Mielec concern (complete stabiliser, all movable aerodynamic surfaces and engine pylons, and the entire wing will be built in Poland from 1980).
Notes: The first wide-body airliner of Soviet design, the Il-86 has been evolved under the supervision of General Designer G. V. Novozhilov and is intended for use on both domestic and international high-density routes. Four are to be supplied to LOT Polish Airlines in 1980—81 in barter for the initial subcontracts in the IL-86 programme undertaken by WSK-Mielec. A long-haul version of the Il-86 was envisaged with imported General Electric CF6-50 turbofans, but negotiations for the importation of these engines into the Soviet Union broke down in 1978, and the current lack of suitable Soviet engines would suggest that the long-haul project has now been shelved.

ILYUSHIN IL-86 (CAMBER)

Dimensions: Span, 157 ft 8½ in (48,06 m); length, 195 ft 4 in (59,54 m); height, 51 ft 10½ in (15,81 m); wing area, 3,550 sq ft (329,80 m²).

131

JUROM (IAR 93) ORAO

Countries of Origin: Jugoslavia and Romania.
Type: Single-seat tactical fighter and two-seat operational trainer.
Power Plant: Two 4,000 lb (1 814 kg) Rolls-Royce Viper 632-41 turbojets.
Performance: (Estimated) Max. speed, 700 mph (1 126 km/h) or Mach 0·92 at sea level, 627 mph (1 010 km/h) or Mach 0·95 at 40,000 ft (12 190 m); radius of action with 4,410-lb (2 000-kg) warload (LO-LO-LO), 155 mls (250 km), (HI-LO-HI), 280 mls (450 km); initial climb, 17,700 ft/min (90 m/sec); service ceiling, 44,290 ft (13 500 m).
Weights: (Estimated) Empty equipped, 9,700 lb (4 400 kg); max. take-off, 19,840 lb (9 000 kg).
Armament: Two 30-mm cannon and up to 4,410 lb (2 000 kg) of ordnance on five external stations.
Status: First of three prototypes flown in August 1974, the second prototype being a tandem two-seater, and nine preseries examples followed during 1977–78, with first production aircraft reportedly delivered 1978–79.
Notes: The Orao (Eagle) has been developed jointly by the Jugoslav (SOKO) and Romanian (CIAR) industries (thus being known by the achronym JuRom), the Romanian industry designating it IAR 93. The Jugoslav SOKO organisation is airframe team leader and is responsible for final assembly of Jugoslav– and Romanian-manufactured components, but the programme is reportedly running some two years behind schedule and the SOKO/CIAR team is understood to be engaged in preliminary development of a single-engined derivative powered by the Pratt & Whitney TF30 turbofan. It is probable that such a development will retain little commonality with the Orao.

132

JUROM (IAR 93) ORAO

Dimensions: (Estimated) Span, 24 ft 7 in (7,50 m); length,
42 ft 8 in (13,00 m); height, 12 ft 1½ in (3,70 m); wing area,
193·75 sq ft (18,00 m²).

LEARAVIA LEAR FAN 2100

Country of Origin: USA.

Type: Light business executive transport.

Power Plant: Two 825 shp (flat rated at 650 shp) Pratt & Whitney PT6B-35F turboshafts.

Performance: (Estimated) Max. speed, 420 mph (676 km/h) at 30,000 ft (9 145 m); max. cruise, 400 mph (644 km/h) at 30,000 ft (9 145 m); con. cruise, 350 mph (563 km/h) at 41,000 ft (12 495 m); range (at econ. cruise), 1,500 mls (2 414 km) with max. payload (1,900 lb/862 kg), 2,300 mls (3 700 km) with 500-lb (237 kg) payload.

Weights: Empty, 3,650 lb (1 656 kg); max. take-off, 7,200 lb (3 266 kg).

Accommodation: Pilot and co-pilot/passenger in side-by-side seats on flight deck and up to seven passengers in main cabin.

Status: First of two flying prototypes of the Lear Fan is scheduled to commence its test programme late August 1980, with production deliveries scheduled for late 1981. By the beginning of 1980, firm orders had been placed for 80 aircraft.

Notes: The Lear Fan 2100 is radical both in concept and construction. Both fuselage and wing are of graphite/epoxy construction (woven graphite impregnated with epoxy resin), all fuel is carried in integral wing tanks and the two turboshafts are located side-by-side in the rear fuselage driving a single pusher propeller via a gearbox drive train. Its finely-contoured computer-designed fuselage is, according to LearAvia, aerodynamically the most efficient profile ever used in general aviation.

LEARAVIA LEAR FAN 2100

Dimensions: Span, 39 ft 4 in (11,99 m); length, 39 ft 8 in (12,09 m); height, 11 ft 6 in (3,50 m)

LET L-410 UVP TURBOLET

Country of Origin: Czechoslovakia.
Type: Light utility transport and feederliner.
Power Plant: Two 740 ehp Walter M-601 B turboprops.
Performance: Max. cruising speed, 227 mph (365 km/h); econ. cruise, 186 mph (300 km/h) range (at max. cruise with 30 min reserves), 646 mls (1 040 km) at 9,845 ft (3 000 m).
Weights: Empty, 8,150 lb (3 700 kg); max. take-off, 12,555 lb (5 700 kg).
Accommodation: Flight crew of two and standard arrangement in main cabin for 15 passengers. Provision in standard aircraft for rapid conversion to freighter configuration (with a 2,885-lb/1 310-kg payload), for the aeromedical role with six stretchers and five seated casualties, plus medical attendant, as a paratroop transport for up to 14 paratroops and as a fire-control aircraft with accommodation for up to 12 personnel.
Status: The L-410 UVP is the latest development of the Turbolet, the first of four prototypes of which flew on April 16, 1969. Flight development of the L-410 UVP (the suffix letters indicating STOL performance) began in 1977, and current production is intended primarily for Aeroflot (for air taxi use).
Notes: The Turbolet has been in continuous production since 1971, and the L-410 UVP model differs from preceding versions in having a lengthened fuselage, a longer-span wing with spoilers, taller vertical tail surfaces, and other changes. Early models of the Turbolet were powered by the Pratt & Whitney PT6A-27.

136

LET L-410 UVP TURBOLET

Dimensions: Span, 63 ft 9½ in (19,49 m); length, 47 ft 5 in (14,47 m); height, 19 ft 1½ in (5,83 m).

LOCKHEED C-130 HERCULES

Country of Origin: USA.

Type: Medium- to long-range military transport.

Power Plant: Four 4,050 eshp Allison T56-A-7A turboprops.

Performance: (C-130H) Max. speed, 384 mph (618 km/h); max. cruise, 368 mph (592 km/h); econ. cruise, 340 mph (547 km/h); range (with max. payload and 5% plus 30 min reserves), 2,450 mls (3 943 km); max. range, 4,770 mls (7 675 km); initial climb, 1,900 ft/min (9,65 m/sec).

Weights: (C-130H) Empty equipped, 72,892 lb (33 063 kg); max. normal take-off, 155,000 lb (70 310 kg); max. overload, 175,000 lb (79 380 kg).

Accommodation: (C-130H) Flight crew of four and max. of 92 troops, 64 paratroops, or 74 casualty stretchers plus two medical attendants. (C-130K Hercules C Mk. 2) Max. of 128 troops or seven cargo pallets.

Status: The 1,500th Hercules was delivered (to Sudan) on March 13, 1978, this total comprising 998 to US services, 433 to overseas governments and 69 to civil operators. By 1980, production totalled some 1,550 for 46 countries.

Notes: In the autumn of 1978, the UK Ministry of Defence announced its decision to initiate a "stretch" programme for 30 of the RAF's Hercules C. Mk. 1 (C-130K) transports (equivalent to the C-130H). These are to have two fuselage plugs totalling 180 in (4,57 m) similar to those of the commercial L-100-30, and a prototype conversion (being undertaken by the parent company) was accepted by the RAF on December 11, 1979, the remaining conversions being undertaken in the UK during 1980–83 by Marshall. The "stretched" Hercules C Mk 3 for the RAF is illustrated above and opposite.

LOCKHEED C-130 HERCULES

Dimensions (Hercules C Mk. 2) Span, 132 ft 7 in (40,41 m); length, 112 ft 9 in (34,37 m); height, 38 ft 3 in (11,66 m); wing area, 1,745 sq ft (162,12 m²).

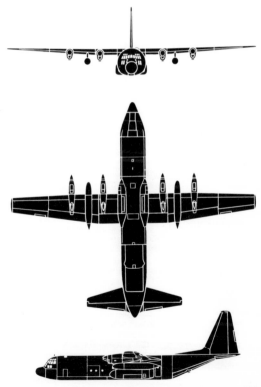

LOCKHEED C-141B STARLIFTER

Country of Origin: USA.

Type: Heavy military strategic transport.

Power Plant: Four 21,000 lb (9525 kg) Pratt & Whitney TF33-P-7 turbofans.

Performance: Max. cruise, 512 mph (824 km/h) at 38,000 ft (11 590 m), or Mach 0·775; range with max. payload (89,096 lb/44 450 kg), 2,650 mls (4 264 km); max. unrefuelled range (59,800 lb/27 150 kg payload), 4,320 mls (6 950 km).

Weights: Operational empty, 149,904 lb (68 056 kg); max. take-off, 343,000 lb (155 580 kg) in weight.

Accommodation: Flight crew of four. Freight hold can accept a total of 13 standard 463L freight pallets totalling 59,800 lb (27 150 kg) in weight.

Status: Sole YC-141B flown on March 24, 1977, and decision announced on June 8, 1978, to convert the USAF's entire fleet of 271 C-141A StarLifters to similar standards as C-141Bs, the modification programme having commenced early 1979, and being scheduled for completion by July 1982.

Notes: The C-141B is a stretched version of the original C-141A StarLifter, 285 examples of which had been built when production terminated in 1968. The conversion, which increases cargo capability by 35%, comprises stretching the fuselage (in two sections—ahead and aft of the wing) by 23 ft 4 in (7,12 m) and adding drag-reducing fillets at the leading and trailing edges of the wing roots. In addition, flight refuelling capability is incorporated in a fairing aft of the cockpit above the fuselage pressure shell. The flight test programme with the YC-141B was completed in July 1977, two months ahead of schedule, and the C-141B programme is claimed to be the equivalent of adding 90 new transport aircraft to the USAF's inventory.

LOCKHEED C-141B STARLIFTER

Dimensions: Span, 159 ft 11 in (48,74 m); length, 168 ft 4 in (51,34 m); height, 39 ft 3 in (11,97 m); wing area, 3,228 sq ft (299,90 m²).

LOCKHEED P-3C ORION

Country of Origin: USA.

Type: Long-range maritime patrol aircraft.

Power Plant: Four 4,910 eshp Allison T56-A-14W turbo-props.

Performance: Max. speed at 105,000 lb (47 625 kg), 473 mph (761 km/h) at 15,000 ft (4 570 m); normal cruise, 397 mph (639 km/h) at 25,000 ft (7 620 m); patrol speed, 230 mph (370 km/h) at 1,500 ft (457 m); loiter endurance (all engines) at 1,500 ft (457 m), 12.3 hours, (two engines), 17 hrs; max. mission radius, 2,530 mls (4 075 km), with 3 hrs on station at 1,500 ft (457 m), 1,933 mls (3 110 km); initial climb, 2,880 ft/min (14,6 m/sec).

Weights: Empty, 61,491 lb (27 890 kg); normal max. take-off, 133,500 lb (60 558 kg); max. overload, 142,000 lb (64 410 kg).

Accommodation: Normal flight crew of 10 of which five housed in tactical compartment. Up to 50 combat troops and 4,000 lb (1 814 kg) of equipment for trooping role.

Armament: Weapons bay can house two Mk 101 depth bombs and four Mk 43, 44 or 46 torpedoes, or eight Mk 54 bombs. External ordnance load of up to 13,713 lb (6 220 kg).

Status: YP-3C prototype flown October 8, 1968, P-3C deliveries commencing to US Navy mid-1969 with some 185 by 1980 against planned procurement (through 1982) of 240. Licence manufacture by Kawasaki of 42 (of 45) for Japanese Maritime Self-Defence Force, six to Iran (as P-3Fs), 10 to the RAAF, 18 for Canada (as CP-140 Auroras) from 1980, the first of these being illustrated above, and 13 for the Netherlands with deliveries commencing in 1981.

Notes: The Canadian version combines the P-3 airframes and engines with the electronic systems of the carrier-based S-3A Viking (see 1978 edition).

LOCKHEED P-3C ORION

Dimensions: Span, 99 ft 8 in (30,37 m); length, 116 ft 10 in (35,61 m); height, 33 ft 8½ in (10,29 m); wing area, 1,300 sq ft (120,77 m²).

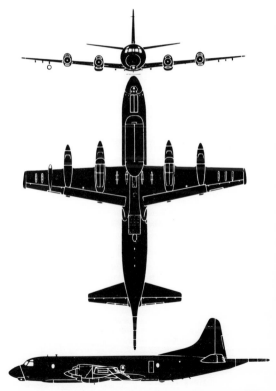

LOCKHEED L-1011-500 TRISTAR

Country of Origin: USA.

Type: Long-haul commercial transport.

Power Plant: Three 48,000 lb (21 772 kg) Rolls-Royce RB.211-524B turbofans.

Performance: (Estimated) Max. cruise, 608 mph (978 km/h) at 31,000 ft (9 450 m); econ. cruise, 567 mph (913 km/h) at 31,000 ft (9 450 m), or Mach 0·84; range (with full passenger payload), 6,053 mls (9 742 km), (with space limited max. payload), 4,855 mls (7 815 km).

Weights: Operational empty, 240,139 lb (108 925 kg); max. take-off, 496,000 lb (224 982 kg).

Accommodation: Basic flight crew of three and mixed-class arrangement for 222 economy (nine-abreast seating) and 24 first (six-abreast seating) class passengers.

Status: First L-1011-500 (for British Airways) flown on October 16, 1978, this version of the TriStar also having been ordered by AeroPeru, Air Canada, BWIA, Delta, LTU, Pan American and Air Portugal. Total of 230 (all versions) on order (plus 71 options) at beginning of 1980, when monthly production rate was moving up from 2·0 to 2·5 aircraft.

Notes: The TriStar 500 is a shorter-fuselage longer-range derivative of the basic L-1011-1 transcontinental version of the TriStar, a 62-in (157,5-cm) section being removed from the fuselage aft of the wing and a 100-in (254-cm) section forward. Versions with the standard fuselage are the L-1011-1, -100 and -200, the last-mentioned model (see 1977 edition) featuring additional centre section fuel tankage and -524 in place of -22B or -22F engines of 42,000 (19 050 kg) and 43,500 lb (19 730 kg) respectively. The -400 is version similar to the -500 but with the -1 wing and smaller engines.

LOCKHEED L-1011-500 TRISTAR

Dimensions: Span, 164 ft 3½ in (50,07 m) ; length, 164 ft 2 in (50,04 m) ; height, 55 ft 4 in (16,87 m) ; wing area, 3,541 sq ft (328,96 m²).

McDONNELL DOUGLAS DC-9
SUPER 80

Country of Origin: USA.

Type: Short- to medium-haul commercial transport.

Power Plant: Two 19,250 lb (8 730 kg) Pratt & Whitney JT8D-209 turbofans (alternative rating of 18,500 lb/8 400 kg).

Performance: Max. cruising speed, 577 mph (928 km/h) at 27,000 ft (8 230 m); long-range cruise, 508 mph (817 km/h) at 35,000 ft (10 670 m); range (with max. payload), 1,508 mls (2 427 km) at 523 mph (841 km/h) at 33,000 ft (10 060 m); max. range (with 22,760 lb/10 324 kg), 3,167 mls (5 095 km) at 508 mph (817 km/h) at 35,000 ft (10 670 m).

Weights: Operational empty, 78,666 lb (35 683 kg); max. take-off, 140,000 lb (63 503 kg).

Accommodation: Flight crew of two and typical mixed-class accommodation for 23 first-class and 137 economy-class passengers, or 155 all economy or 172 commuter-type layouts with five-abreast seating.

Status: The first Super 80 was flown on October 18, 1979, with customer deliveries (to Swissair) scheduled for spring 1980. By the beginning of 1980, 10 airlines had announced orders for 75 Super 80s (plus options on 24), approximately 1,045 DC-9s of all types having been ordered with some 930 delivered.

Notes: The newest and largest member of the DC-9 family with, by comparison with what was previously the largest, the Series 50 (see 1978 edition), a 14 ft 3 in (4,34 m) fuselage "stretch" and an extended wing, larger tailplane, new leading-edge wing slat and uprated engines. A derivative currently being proposed is the Super 80SF combining the wing and engines of the Super 80 with the fuselage of the Series 40 (see 1972 edition).

McDONNELL DOUGLAS DC-9 SUPER 80

Dimensions: Span, 107 ft 10 in (32,85 m); length, 147 ft 10 in (45,08 m); height, 29 ft 4 in (8,93 m); wing area, 1,279 sq ft (118,8 m²).

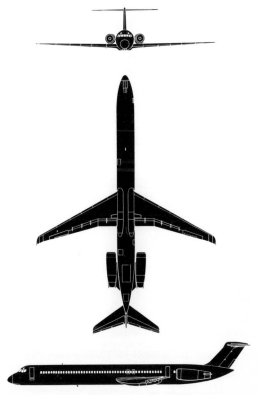

McDONNELL DOUGLAS DC-10 SERIES 30

Country of Origin: USA.

Type: Medium-range commercial transport.

Power Plant: Three 52,500 lb (23 814 kg) General Electric CF6-50C1 turbofans.

Performance: Max. cruise (at 400,000 lb/181 440 kg), 594 mph (956 km/h) at 31,000 ft (9 450 m); long-range cruise, 540 mph (870 km/h) at 31,000 ft (9 450 m); range (with max. payload), 6,195 mls (9 970 km) at 575 mph (925 km/h) at 31,000 ft (9 450 m); max. range, 7,400 mls (11 910 km) at 540 mph (870 km/h).

Weights: Operational empty, 261,459 lb (118 597 kg); max. take-off, 572,000 lb (259 457 kg).

Accommodation: Flight crew of three plus provision on flight deck for two supernumerary crew. Typical mixed-class accommodation for 225–270 passengers. Max. authorised passenger accommodation, 380 (plus crew of 11).

Status: First DC-10 (Series 10) flown August 29,1970, with first Series 30 (46th DC-10 built) flying June 21, 1972, being preceded on February 28, 1972, by first Series 40. Orders for DC-10s totalled 350 at beginning of 1980, with 41 to be delivered during year and 300th in January of that year.

Notes: The DC-10 Series 30 and 40 have identical fuselages to the DC-10 Series 10 (see 1972 edition) and 15, but whereas these last-mentioned versions are domestic models, the Series 30 and 40 are intercontinental models and differ in power plant, weights and wing details, and in the use of three main undercarriage units. The Series 40 has 53,000 lb (24 040 kg) Pratt & Whitney JT9D-59A turbofans but is otherwise similar to the Series 30. The Series 10 and 15 have 41,000 lb (18 597 kg) CF6-6s and 46,500 lb (21 090 kg) CF6-45B2s respectively.

McDONNELL DOUGLAS DC-10 SERIES 30

Dimensions: Span, 165 ft 4 in (50,42 m); length, 181 ft 4¾ in (55,29 m); height, 58 ft 0 in (17,68 m); wing area, 3,921·4 sq ft (364,3 m²).

McDONNELL DOUGLAS AV-8B

Country of Origin: USA.

Type: Single-seat V/STOL strike and reconnaissance fighter.

Power Plant: One 21,500 lb (9 760 kg) Rolls-Royce F402-RR-402 vectored-thrust turbofan.

Performance: (Estimated) Max. speed, 720 mph (1 160 km/h) at 1,000 ft (305 m), or Mach 0·95, (with typical external ordnance), 640 mph (1 030 km/h) at 1,000 ft (305 m), or Mach 0·85; VTO radius (with 1,800-lb/817-kg payload), 230 mls (370 km); STO radius (with 6,000-lb/2 724-kg payload), 460 mls (740 km), (with 2,000-lb/908-kg payload), 920 mls (1 480 km); ferry range, 2,966 mls (4 774 km).

Weights: Operational empty, 12,400 lb (5 265 kg); max. vertical take-off, 18,850 lb (8 558 kg); max. short take-off, 27,950 lb (12 690 kg); max. take-off, 29,550 lb (13 416 kg).

Armament: Two 30-mm cannon in detachable ventral pod as alternative to centreline stores pylon. Seven external pylons (one fuselage and six wing) with combined capacity of 8,000 lb (3 632 kg).

Status: First of two YAV-8Bs (converted from AV-8A Harrier airframes) was flown on November 9, 1978. Full-scale development was originally scheduled to commence in January 1979, this calling for the construction of four new AV-8Bs with the first of these flying mid-1981, full-scale production following from 1983 against US Marine Corps requirements for 336 aircraft. However, the omission of funding for the programme by the Department of Defense in FY80 procurement planning in favour of additional Hornets and the considerable controversy that ensued has left the future of the AV-8B uncertain.

Notes: The AV-8B is a derivative of the Harrier alias AV-8A (see pages 36–37) with a new graphite epoxy composite wing of supercritical section, redesigned air intakes, various lift improvement devices and new avionics.

McDONNELL DOUGLAS AV-8B

Dimensions: Span, 30 ft 4 in (9,25 m); length, 42 ft 10 in (13,08 m); height, 11 ft 3 in (3,43 m); wing area, 230 sq ft (21,37 m²).

McDONNELL DOUGLAS F-15C EAGLE

Country of Origin: USA.

Type: Single-seat air superiority fighter (F-15C) and two-seat operational trainer (F-15D).

Power Plant: Two (approx) 25,000 lb (11 340 kg) reheat Pratt & Whitney F100-PW-100 turbofans.

Performance: Max. speed, 915 mph (1 472 km/h) or Mach 1·5 at sea level, 1,650 mph (2 655 km/h) or Mach 2·5 at 36,090 ft (11 000 m); tactical radius (combat air patrol), 1,305 mls (2 100 km); ferry range, 3,475 mls (5 592 km).

Weights: Empty equipped, 26,442 lb (11 994 kg); loaded (clean), 38,840 lb (17 618 kg); max. take-off, 68,000 lb (30 870 kg).

Armament: One 20-mm M-61A-1 rotary cannot with 950 rounds and (intercept mission) four AIM-9L Sidewinder and four AIM-7F Sparrow AAMs. Five stores stations can lift up to 15,000 lb (6 804 kg) of ordnance.

Status: The second major production version of the single-seat Eagle, the F-15C flew for the first time on February 26, 1979, production of this model supplanting the F-15A from mid-1980, the two-seat equivalent F-15D simultaneously supplanting the F-15B. Production of the Eagle exceeded 480 aircraft by the beginning of 1980 to meet planned USAF procurement of 729, plus 25 for Israel, 60 for Saudi Arabia and eight (plus eight in the form of knocked-down assemblies) for Japan. A further 84 F-15Cs (F-15Js) are to be licence-manufactured in Japan.

Notes: The F-15C (and -15D) differs from the F-15A (and -15B) in having increased internal fuel capacity, provision for a further 10,000 lb (4 540 kg) of fuel (or fuel and sensors) and for conformal tanks (FAST packs) on the fuselage sides, plus programmable radar signal processors.

McDONNELL DOUGLAS F-15C Eagle

Dimensions: Span, 42 ft 9¾ in (13,05 m); length, 63 ft 9 in (19,43 m); height, 18 ft 5½ in (5,63 m); wing area, 608 sq ft (56,50 m²).

McDONNELL DOUGLAS F-18A HORNET

Country of Origin: USA.

Type: Single-seat shipboard air superiority fighter and attack aircraft.

Power Plant: Two (approx.) 10,600 lb (4 810 kg) dry and 16,000 lb (7 260 kg) reheat General Electric F404-GE-400 turbofans.

Performance: (Estimated) Max. speed, 1,190+mph (1 915+ km/h) at 36,000 ft (10 970 m) or Mach 1·8+ 915 mph (1 472 km/h) at sea level or Mach 1·2; combat radius (fighter escort mission, internal fuel), 480 mls (770 km), (interdiction mission HI-LO-HI profile with four 1,000-lb/454-kg bombs, two AIM-9 Sidewinders and 1,008 Imp gal/4 584 l external fuel), 670 mls (1 080 km); ferry range, 2,300+ mls (3 700+ km).

Weights: (Estimated) Operational empty, 21,500 lb (9 760 kg); normal loaded (air–air mission, internal fuel), 33,585 lb (15 248 kg); max. take-off, 45,300 lb (20 566 kg).

Armament: One 20-mm multi-barrel M61 cannon and ASMs, bombs, etc, on nine external stations. Max. external load of 19,000 lb (8 618 kg).

Status: First of 11 (nine F-18As and two TF-18As) full-scale development (FSD) aircraft flown November 18, 1978, and last of remaining aircraft scheduled for delivery early 1980. Procurement of 800 production aircraft originally planned for US Navy and USMC, this increased to 1,366 (including 153 TF-18As) early 1979 to permit re-equipment of all 24 of the US Navy's attack squadrons, plus six fighter squadrons, and 12 USMC fighter and 20 attack squadrons, plus 30 aircraft for the TACA (Tactical Airborne Command Aircraft) role.

Notes: The Hornet is a derivative of the Northrop YF-17 (see 1975 edition), of which McDonnell Douglas is team leader with Northrop being responsible for 30% of airframe development and 40% of airframe production.

154

McDONNELL DOUGLAS F-18A HORNET

Dimensions: Span (without missiles), 37 ft 6 in (11,43 m); length, 56 ft 0 in (17,07 m); height, 15 ft 4 in (4,67 m); wing area, 400 sq ft (37,16 m²).

McDONNELL DOUGLAS KC-10A EXTENDER

Country of Origin: USA.

Type: Flight refuelling tanker and cargo aircraft.

Power Plant: Three 52,500 lb (23 814 kg) General Electric CF6-50C1 turbofans.

Performance: (Estimated) Max. speed, 620 mph (998 km/h) at 33,000 ft (10 060 m); max. cruise, 595 mph (957 km/h) at 31,000 ft (9 450 m); long-range cruise, 540 mph (870 km/h) at 31,000 ft (9 450 m); typical refuelling mission, 2,200 mls (3 540 km) from base with 200,000 lb (90 720 kg) of fuel and return; max. range (with 170,000 lb/77 112 kg cargo), 4,370 mls (7 033 km).

Weights: Operational empty (tanker), 239,747 lb (108 749 kg), (cargo configuration), 243,973 lb (110 660 kg); max. take-off, 590 000 lb (267 624 kg).

Accommodation: Flight crew of five plus provision for six seats for additional crew and four bunks for crew rest. Fourteen additional seats for support personnel may be provided in the forward cabin. Alternatively, a larger area can be provided for 55 more support personnel, with necessary facilities, to make total accommodation for 80, including the flight crew.

Status: The first of two KC-10As ordered on 20 November 1978, is scheduled to fly in April 1980 and to be delivered to the USAF in the following October. Incremental orders for the KC-10A (first of which calling for an additional four aircraft was placed in November 1979) are expected to provide the USAF with a fleet of 20 aircraft by late 1983.

Notes: The Extender is a tanker/cargo derivative of the commercial DC-10 Srs 30 (see pages 148–149).

McDONNELL DOUGLAS KC-10A EXTENDER

Dimensions: Span, 165 ft 4 in (50,42 m); length, 182 ft 3 in (55,55 m); height, 58 ft 1 in (17,70 m); wing area, 3,647 sq ft (338,8 m²).

MIKOYAN MIG-23MF (FLOGGER-B)

Country of Origin: USSR.

Type: Single-seat (MiG-23MF) interceptor and (MiG-23BM) strike fighter.

Power Plant: One 17,635 lb (8 000 kg) dry and 25,350 lb (11 500 kg) reheat Tumansky R-29B turbofan.

Performance: Max. speed, 838 mph (1 350 km/h) at 1,000 ft (305 m) or Mach 1·1, 1,520 mph (2 446 km/h) above 39,370 ft (12 000 m); combat radius (intercept mission with four AAMs and 176 Imp gal/800 l centreline tank), 450–500 mls (725–805 km); max. range (with three 176 Imp gal/800 l drop tanks), 1,400 mls (2 250 km) at 495 mph (795 km/h) or Mach 0·75; ceiling, 60,000 ft (18 300 m).

Weights: Normal loaded (clean), 34,170 lb (15 500 kg); max. take-off, 44,312 lb (20 100 kg).

Armament: One 23-mm twin-barrel GSh-23L cannon plus (MiG-23MF) two AA-7 Apex and two AA-8 Aphid AAMs, or (MiG-23BM) up to 9,920 lb (4 500 kg) of bombs and/or air-to-surface missiles on five external stations.

Status: Prototype MiG-23 first flown early 1967, and initial intercept model (MiG-23S) phased into SoVAF service from 1971. Current models include MiG-23MF, MiG-23BM and BN, and two-seat MiG-23UM.

Notes: MiG-23BM differs from MiG-23MF Flogger-B (illustrated above and opposite) in having a redesigned nose with the *High Lark* intercept radar replaced by radar ranging and a laser ranger. Export versions of the MF and BM (with downgraded equipment) are known as the Flogger-E and -F respectively, and production of the MF and BN versions is to be undertaken in India 1982–83.

MIKOYAN MIG-23MF (FLOGGER-B)

Dimensions: (Estimated) Span (17 deg sweep), 46 ft 9 in (14,25 m), (72 deg sweep), 27 ft 6 in (8,38 m); length (including probe), 55 ft 1½ in (16,80 m); wing area, 293·4 sq ft (27,26 m²).

MIKOYAN MIG-25 (FOXBAT)

Country of Origin: USSR.

Type: Single-seat interceptor (Foxbat-A), high-altitude reconnaissance aircraft (Foxbat-B and -D) and two-seat conversion trainer (Foxbat-C).

Power Plant: Two 20,500 lb (9 300 kg) dry and 27,120 lb (12 300 kg) reheat Tumansky R-31 turbojets.

Performance: (Foxbat-A) Max (dash) speed (with four AAMs), 1,850 mph (2 980 km/h) above 36,000 ft (10 970 m) or Mach 2·8; max speed at sea level, 650 mph (1 045 km/h) or Mach 0·85; initial climb, 40,950 ft/min (208 m/sec); time to 36,000 ft (10 970 m), 2·5 min; service ceiling, 80,000 ft (24 000 m); mission radius (range-optimised profile), 590 mls (950 km), (dash only), 250 mls (400 km); max. ferry range, 1,600 mls (2,575 m).

Weights: Empty equipped, 44,100 lb (20 000 kg); max. take-off, 77,160 lb (35 000 kg).

Armament: Four AA-5 Ash or AA-6 Acrid AAMs (two infra-red homing and two semi-active radar homing).

Status: MiG-25 entered V-VS service (in Foxbat-A form) in 1970, recce versions following in 1971 (Foxbat-B) and 1973 (Foxbat-D).

Notes: The Foxbat-B and -D differ from the Foxbat-A (illustrated) in having a new nose section, the -B having a battery of five cameras and SLAR (side-looking radar) and the -D having the cameras omitted (being a dedicated electronic intelligence version) with a larger SLAR and other intelligence gathering equipment. An advanced interceptor derivative with tandem seating for a crew of two, uprated R-31F engines and new radar possessing lookdown-shootdown capability was under evaluation at the beginning of 1980.

MIKOYAN MIG-25 (FOXBAT)

Dimensions: Span, 45 ft 9 in (13,94 m); length, 73 ft 2 in (22,30 m); height, 18 ft 4½ in (5,60 m); wing area, 602·8 sq ft (56,00 m²).

MIKOYAN MIG-27 (FLOGGER-D)

Country of Origin: USSR.

Type: Single-seat tactical strike fighter.

Power Plant: One 17,635 lb (8 000 kg) dry and 25,350 lb (11 500 kg) reheat Tumansky R-29B turbofan.

Performance: Max. speed, 838 mph (1 350 km/h) at 1,000 ft (305 m) or Mach 1·1, 990 mph (1 595 km/h) or Mach 1·5 above 39,370 ft (12 000 m); combat radius (LO-LO-LO mission profile with 176 Imp gal/800 l centreline tank and six 1,102-lb/500-kg bombs), 350 mls (560 km), (HI-LO-HI profile), 550 mls (885 km); max. range (with three 176 Imp gal/800 1 drop tanks), 1,400 mls.

Weights: Normal loaded (clean), 34,170 lb (15 500 kg); max. take-off, 44,312 lb (20 100 kg).

Armament: One 23-mm six-barrel rotary cannon and six 1,102-lb (500-kg) bombs, or mix of AS-7 Kerry ASMs, rocket pods and bombs.

Status: Believed to have entered SovAF service in 1974.

Notes: Dedicated tactical strike derivative of MiG-23, sharing redesigned, drooped nose (to improve ground target acquisition) incorporating laser ranger with MiG-23BM, but having simplified, fixed-ramp air intakes, shorter reheat nozzle, broader after centre fuselage (housing revised undercarriage for grass-field operation), hardpoints on moving portion of wing and a Gatling-type cannon.

MIKOYAN MIG-27 (FLOGGER-D)

Dimensions: (Estimated) Span (17 deg sweep), 46 ft 9 in (14,25 m), (72 deg sweep), 27 ft 6 in (8,38 m); length (including probe), 54 ft 0 in (16,46 m); wing area, 293·4 sq ft (27,26 m²).

MITSUBISHI F-1

Country of Origin: Japan.

Type: Single-seat close air support fighter.

Power Plant: Two 4,710 lb (2 136 kg) dry and 7,070 lb (3 207 kg) reheat Ishikawajima-Harima TF40-IHI-801A (Rolls-Royce/Turboméca Adour) turbofans.

Performance: Max. speed, 1,056 mph (1 700 km/h) at 40,000 ft (12 190 m), or Mach 1·6; combat radius (internal fuel only plus four Sidewinder AAMs), 173 mls (278 km), lo-lo-lo (with eight 500-lb/226,8-kg bombs and two 180 Imp gal/820 l drop tanks), 218 mls (351 km), HI-LO-HI (with ASM-1 anti-shipping missiles and one 180 Imp gal/820 l drop tank), 346 mls (556 km); max. ferry range, 1,785 mls (2 870 km); max. climb, 35,000 ft/min (177,8 m/sec).

Weights: Operational empty, 14,017 lb (6 358 kg); max. take-off, 30,146 lb (13 674 kg).

Armament: One 20-mm Vulcan JM-61 multi-barrel cannon. Five external stores stations for up to 8,000 lb (3 629 kg) of ordnance. Detachable multiple ejector racks may be fitted for up to 12 500-lb (226,8-kg) bombs. Wingtip attachment points for two or four Sidewinder or Mitsubishi AAM-1 air-to-air missiles. Two Mitsubishi ASM-1 anti-shipping missiles may be carried.

Status: Two prototypes (adapted from T-2 airframes) flown on June 3 and June 7, 1975, with first production F-1 following on June 16, 1977. Sixty-nine (of planned procurement of 77) ordered by beginning of 1980, with 44 scheduled for delivery by April 1980.

Notes: The F-1 is replacing the F-86F Sabre in the Air Self-Defence Force's two-squadron 3rd Air Wing and one squadron in the 8th Air Wing. The airframe is essentially similar to that of the T-2 trainer, the two being assembled on a single line.

164

MITSUBISHI F-1

Dimensions: Span, 25 ft 10¼ in (7,88 m); length, 58 ft 7 in (17,86 m); height, 14 ft 4¾ in (4,39 m); wing area, 228 sq ft (21,18 m²).

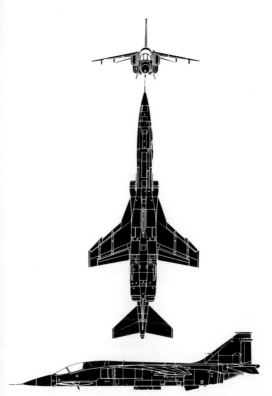

MITSUBISHI MU-300 DIAMOND I

Country of Origin: Japan.

Type: Light business executive transport.

Power Plant: Two 2,500 lb (1 134 kg) Pratt & Whitney JT15D-4 turbofans.

Performance: Max. operating speed, 500 mph (804 km/h) at 30,000 ft (9 145 m); typical cruise, 472 mph (760 km/h) at 39,000 ft (11 890 m); long-range cruise, 432 mph (695 km/h) at 39,000 ft (11 890 m); initial climb, 3,000 ft/min (15,2 m/sec); max. range (four passengers), 1,800 mls (2 896 km).

Weights: Empty equipped, 8,300 lb (3 764 kg); max. take-off, 13,890 lb (6 300 kg).

Accommodation: Pilot and co-pilot/passenger on flight deck and seven–nine passengers in main cabin.

Status: First of two prototypes flown on August 29, 1978, with second following in December 1978. The first four production aircraft are being assembled and flown by Mitsubishi at Nagoya. Thereafter, Mitsubishi will ship sets of components to the Mitsubishi facility at San Angelo, Texas, for assembly and flight testing. The first customer deliveries are scheduled for early 1981.

Notes: Intended as a successor to the MU-2 Solitaire and Marquise turboprop-powered light business executive transports, the Diamond is of thoroughly conventional structural design, the wing geometry being computer-generated and emphasis being placed on economy of operation, low noise level and good field performance, the last-mentioned attribute being obtained by means of large-span Fowler-type flaps, double-slotted on their inboard positions. Lateral control is by means of spoilers which may be used simultaneously as speed brakes.

MITSUBISHI MU-300 DIAMOND I

Dimensions: Span, 43 ft 5 in (13,23 m); length, 48 ft 4 in (14,73 m); height, 13 ft 9 in (4,19 m); wing area, 241·4 sq ft (22,43 m²).

NORTHROP F-5E (RF-5E) TIGER II

Country of Origin: USA.

Type: Single-seat air superiority and (RF-5E) tactical reconnaissance fighter.

Power Plant: Two 3,500 lb (1 588 kg) dry and 5,000 lb (2 268 kg) reheat General Electric J85-GE-21 turbojets.

Performance: Max. speed (at 13,220 lb/5 997 kg), 1,056 mph (1 700 km/h) or Mach 1·6 at 36,090 ft (11 000 m), 760 mph (1 223 km/h) or Mach 1·0 at sea level, (with wingtip missiles), 990 mph (1 594 km/h) or Mach 1·5 at 36,090 ft (11 000 m); combat radius (internal fuel), 173 mls (278 km), (with 229 Imp gal/1 041 l drop tank), 426 mls (686 km); initial climb (at 13,220 lb/5 997 kg), 31,600 ft/min (160,53 m/sec); combat ceiling, 53,500 ft (16 305 m).

Weights: Take-off (wingtip launching rail configuration), 15,400 lb (6 985 kg); max. take-off, 24,083 lb (10 924 kg).

Armament: (RF-5E) One or (F-5E) two 20-mm M-39 cannon and two wingtip-mounted AIM-9 Sidewinder AAMs. Up to 7,000 lb (3 175 kg) of ordnance may be carried on five stations for the attack role.

Status: First F-5E flown August 11, 1972 and first deliveries February 1973. First RF-5E flown January 29, 1979. Total of 1,028 Tiger II series aircraft (F-5E and two-seat F-5F) had been delivered by the beginning of 1980 when production was running at five–six per month.

Notes: The RF-5E (illustrated) is a tactical reconnaissance version of the F-5E dedicated fighter, with armament reduced by one cannon and a lengthened nose with 26 cu ft (0,74 m³) space for cameras and other sensors carried on quick-change platforms. The two-seat F-5F conversion trainer, which first flew on September 25, 1974, is produced in parallel.

168

NORTHROP RF-5E TIGER II

Dimensions: Span, 26 ft 8½ in (8,14 m); length, 48 ft 2½ in (14,89 m); height, 13 ft 4 in (4,06 m); wing area, 186·2 sq ft (17,29 m²).

PANAVIA TORNADO F. MK. 2

Country of Origin: United Kingdom.

Power Plant: Two 8,000 lb (3 623 kg) dry and 15,000 lb (6 810 kg) reheat Turbo-Union RB. 199-34R-04 Mk. 101 (Improved) Turbofans.

Performance: (Estimated) Max. speed (clean) 840 mph (1 350 km/h) at 500 ft (150 m) or Mach 1·1, 1,450 mph (2 333 km/h) at 36,090 ft (11 000 m) or Mach 2·2; typical mission (with two external subsonic 330 Imp gal/1 500 l tanks), loiter for 2·0–2·5 hrs plus 10 min combat at 250–450 mls (560–725 km) from base; ferry range (full internal and max external fuel), 2,000+ mls (3 220+ km).

Weights: Max. take-off (four Skyflash and two Sidewinder AAMs plus two 330 Imp/gal/1 500 l external tanks), 52,000 lb (23 587 kg).

Armament: One 27-mm Mauser cannon, two AIM-9L Sidewinder AAMs on inboard sides of swivelling wing pylons and four BAe Sky Flash AAMs in paired and staggered semi-recessed housings under fuselage.

Status: First of three prototype Tornado F. Mk. 2s flown on October 27, 1979, with second and third following during course of 1980. RAF requirement for 165 aircraft with initial operational capability to be achieved by end of 1984.

Notes: The Tornado F. Mk. 2 is a UK-only derivative of the multi-national (UK, Federal Germany and Italy) multi-role fighter (see 1978 edition) with Foxhunter intercept radar, more fuel in lengthened fuselage and a retractable air refuelling probe replacing the starboard cannon. Eighty per cent commonality with the multi-role version is retained.

170

PANAVIA TORNADO F. MK. 2

Dimensions: Span (max.), 45 ft 7¼ in (13,90 m), (min.), 28 ft 2½ in (8,59 m); length, 59 ft 3 in (18,06 m); wing area, 322·9 sq ft (30,00 m²).

PARTENAVIA P.68C

Country of Origin: Italy.
Type: Light transport aircraft.
Power Plant: Two 200 hp Avco Lycoming 10-360-A1B6 four-cylinder horizontally-opposed engines.
Performance: Max. speed, 200 mph (322 km/h) at sea level; max. cruise, 191 mph (308 km/h) at 7,500 ft (2 286 m) at 75 per cent power; initial climb, 1,600 ft/min (8,1 m/sec); service ceiling, 20,000 ft (6 100 m); max. range, 1,267 mls (2 038 km).
Weights: Typical empty, 2,797 lb (1 270 kg); max. take-off, 4,387 lb (1 990 kg).
Accommodation: Seating for seven persons in cabin, including pilot, in two rows of two seats and a rear bench for three persons. Two stretchers may be carried when all passenger seats are removed.
Status: A total of 220 P.68s (all versions) had been delivered by the beginning of 1980, when production was running at five–six aircraft monthly, flight development of the latest model, the P.68C, having commenced early in 1979.
Notes: This model of the P.68 features integral wing tanks of increased capacity, a marginally lengthened nose to facilitate installation of weather radar, some aerodynamic refinements and is offered with normally aspirated (P.68C) and turbo-supercharged (P.68TC) Engines. Other current developments of the basic design include the P.68TP with de-rated Allison 250-B17B turboprops (see 1979 edition) which is being developed in collaboration with Aeritalia, and the "stretched" P.68 Major providing seating for eight–nine passengers.

PARTENAVIA P.68C

Dimensions: Span, 39 ft 4½ in (12,00 m); length, 31 ft 0 in (9,45 m); height, 11 ft 1¾ in (3,40 m); wing area, 200 sq ft (18,60 m²).

PILATUS PC-7 TURBO TRAINER

Country of Origin: Switzerland.

Type: Tandem two-seat basic trainer.

Power Plant: One 550 shp (flat rated from 650 shp) Pratt & Whitney PT6A-25A turboprop.

Performance: (At 4,189 lb/1 900 kg) Max. speed, 239 mph (385 km/h) at sea level, 264 mph (425 km/h) at 16,405 ft (5 000 m); cruise, 186 mph (300 km/h) at sea level, 205 mph (330 km/h) at 16,405 ft (5 000 m); max. range (at 40% power with 5% plus 20 min reserve), 777 mls (1 250 km); initial climb, 2,008 ft/min (10,2 m/sec).

Weights: Empty, 2,866 lb (1 300 kg); max. take-off (clean), 4,189 lb (1 900 kg), (external stores), 5,952 lb (2 700 kg).

Armament: Six wing hardpoints permit external loads up to maximum of 5,952 lb (2 700 kg).

Status: First of two PC-7 prototypes flown on April 12, 1966, and first production example flown July 1978. Initial production batch of 35 commenced in 1977, with follow-on batches laid down in 1978 and 1979. More than 170 on order for six air forces (including Bolivia, Burma, Guatemala, Iraq and Mexico) by the beginning of 1980, when production rate was running at four per month and a fifth every third month, with approximately 40 aircraft delivered.

Notes: Derived from the piston-engined P-3 basic trainer, the prototypes being conversions of the original P-3 prototype and a series production P-3-05, the PC-7 has undergone extensive structural redesign in its production form and it is anticipated that this type will eventually be adopted by the Swiss *Flugwaffe* which has a requirement for 50–60 aircraft in this category. Two PC-7s have been delivered to the *Flugwaffe* (during 1979) for an extended operational evaluation.

PILATUS PC-7 TURBO TRAINER

Dimensions: Span, 34 ft $1\frac{1}{2}$ in (10,40 m); length, 31 ft $11\frac{7}{8}$ in (9,75 m); height, 10 ft $6\frac{1}{3}$ in (3,21 m); wing area, 178·68 sq ft (16,60 m²).

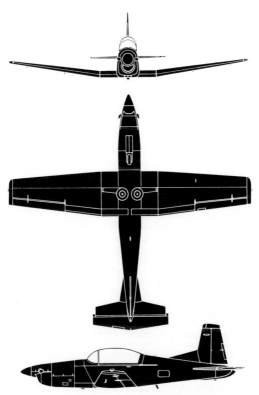

PILATUS BRITTEN-NORMAN
BN2B ISLANDER

Country of Origin: United Kingdom.

Type: Light utility transport.

Power Plant: Two (BN2B-26/27) 260 hp Avco Lycoming O-540-E4C5 or (BN2B-20/21) 300 hp I0-540-K1B5 six-cylinder horizontally-opposed engines.

Performance: (BN2B-20) Max. speed, 180 mph (290 km/h) at sea level; cruise (75% power), 164 mph (264 km/h) at 700 ft (215 m), (67% power), 158 mph (254 km/h) at 9,000 ft (2 745 m), (59% power), 152 mph (244 km/h) at 12,000 ft (3 660 m); range (75% power), 639 mls (1 028 km), (at 59% power), 706 mls (1 136 km); initial climb, 1,130 ft/min (5,74 m/sec); service ceiling, 18,000 ft (5 485 m).

Weights: Empty weight (standard equipment), 4,043 lb (1 834 kg); max. take-off, 6,600 lb (2 994 kg).

Accommodation: Flight crew of one or two and up to nine passengers (one beside pilot and four double seats).

Status: Prototype Islander flown on June 12, 1965, and first production aircraft on August 20, 1966. Approximately 1,020 had been ordered by beginning of 1980, at which time some 990 had been delivered and combined production in UK and Romania was running at 10–12 monthly.

Notes: BN2B is current production standard Islander with two different engines and optional wingtip auxiliary fuel tank extensions (BN2B-21 and -27).

PILATUS BRITTEN-NORMAN BN2B ISLANDER

Dimensions: Span, 49 ft 0 in (14,94 m); length, 35 ft 7¾ in (10,86 m); height, 13 ft 8¾ in (4,18 m); wing area, 325 sq ft (30,19 m²).

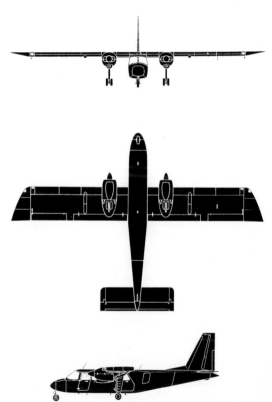

PIPER PA-38 TOMAHAWK

Country of Origin: USA.

Type: Side-by-side two-seat primary trainer.

Power Plant: One 112 bhp Avco Lycoming O-235-L2C four-cylinder horizontally-opposed engine.

Performance: Max. speed, 130 mph (209 km/h) at sea level; cruise (75% power), 125 mph (202 km/h) at 8,800 ft (2 680 m), (65% power), 117 mph (189 km/h) at 11,500 ft (3 505 m); range (with 45 min reserve), 463 mls (745 km) at 75% power, 500 mls (807 km) at 65% power; initial climb, 700 ft/min (3,55 m/sec); service ceiling, 12,850 ft (3 917 m).

Weights: Empty equipped, 1,064 lb (483 kg); max. take-off, 1,670 lb (757 kg).

Status: The PA-38 Tomahawk trainer was announced in October 1977, and customer deliveries commenced early in 1978, and some 2,000 having been delivered by the beginning of 1979. Production of the Tomahawk was averaging 60 monthly at the beginning of 1980.

Notes: Placing emphasis on simplicity of maintenance and low operating costs, the Tomahawk incorporates a high degree of component interchangeability and several design features considered innovative in aircraft of its category. Like the Beechcraft Skipper (see pages 50–51), with which the new Piper trainer is directly competitive, the Tomahawk employs a T-tail, which is claimed to afford greater stability and more positive rudder control, and its high aspect ratio wing of constant chord and thickness utilises a NASA Whitcomb aerofoil.

178

PIPER PA-38 TOMAHAWK

Dimensions: Span, 34 ft 0 in (10,36 m); length, 23 ft 1¼ in (7,04 m); height, 8 ft 7½ in (2,63 m); wing area, 125 sq ft (11,61 m²).

PIPER PA-42 CHEYENNE III

Country of Origin: USA.

Type: Light business executive transport.

Power Plant: Two 680 shp (de-rated from 850 shp) Pratt & Whitney (Canada) PT6A-41 turboprops.

Performance: Max. cruise, 330 mph (532 km/h) at 15,000 ft (4 570 m), 347 mph (558 km/h) at 20,000 ft (6 095 m); max. range, 1,900 mls (3 058 km) at 15,000 ft (4 570 m), 2,050 mls (3,300 km) at 25,000 ft (7 620 m); initial climb, 2,400 ft/min (12,2 m/sec); service ceiling, 30,500 ft (9 295 m).

Weights: Empty equipped, 6,160 lb (2 794 kg).; max. take-off, 11,000 lb (4 990 kg).

Accommodation: Flight crew of one or two on separate flight deck with six—eleven passengers in main cabin.

Status: First production PA-42 flown mid-1978, customer deliveries having been delayed until early 1980 to permit introduction of 36-in (91,44 cm) fuselage "stretch". A production rate of 7—8 monthly is anticipated by late 1980.

Notes: The original PA-31T Cheyenne prototype flew on August 20, 1969, with customer deliveries commencing in 1974. this initial model currently being offered as the Cheyenne I with 500 shp PT6A-11s and as the Cheyenne II with 620 shp PT6A-28s. The PA-42 Cheyenne III is an extensively redesigned model with more powerful engines, enlarged overall dimensions and a tail of T-type.

PIPER PA-42 CHEYENNE III

Dimensions: Span, 47 ft 8$\frac{1}{8}$ in (14,53 m) length, 41 ft 0 in (12,50 m); height, 11 ft 9$\frac{1}{2}$ in (3,61 m); wing area, 293 sq ft (27,20 m²).

PIPER PA-44 SEMINOLE

Country of Origin: USA.

Type: Light cabin monoplane.

Power Plant: Two 180 hp Avco Lycoming O-360-E1AD four-cylinder horizontally-opposed engines.

Performance: Max. speed, 192 mph (309 km/h) at sea level; cruise (75% power), 186 mph (300 km/h), (65% power), 178 mph (286 km/h), (55% power), 170 mph (273 km/h); range (with 45 min reserve), 820 mls (1 321 km) at 75% power, 890 mls (1 435 km) at 65% power, 960 mls (1 546 km) at 55% power; initial climb, 1,220 ft/min (6,2 m/sec); service ceiling, 16,000 ft (4 875 m).

Weights: Empty, 2,406 lb (1 091 kg); max. take-off, 3,800 lb (1 723 kg).

Accommodation: Pilot and three passengers in individual seats and 24 cu ft (0.68 m³) baggage compartment.

Status: The prototype PA-44 Seminole flew in May 1976, and initial production deliveries commenced two years later, in May 1978, with some 340 delivered by the beginning of 1980 when production was averaging 13–14 monthly.

Notes: An all-new design intended as a twin-engined trainer for pilots who have previously flown only single-engined aircraft, the Seminole closely resembles the Duchess 76 (see pages 48–49).

PIPER PA-44 SEMINOLE

Dimensions: Span, 38 ft 6½ in (11,75 m); length, 27 ft 7 in (8,41 m); height, 8 ft 6 in (2,59 m).

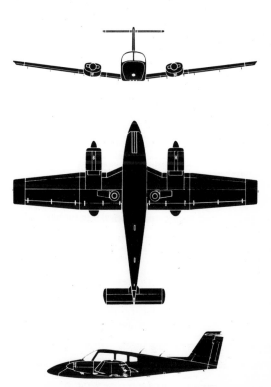

RHEIN-FLUGZEUGBAU FANTRAINER 400

Country of Origin: Federal Germany.
Type: Tandem two-seat basic trainer.
Power Plant: One 420 shp Allison 250-C20B turboshaft driving an integral high bypass fan.
Performance: (At 3,483 lb/1 580 kg) Max. speed, 225 mph (362 km/h) at sea level; max. continuous cruise, 205 mph (330 km/h) at 9,840 ft (3 000 m); range (with 30 min reserves), 460 mls (740 km) at 212 mph (343 km/h) at 2,500 ft (760 m), 575 mls (920 km) at 182 mph (293 km/h) at 5,000 ft (1 525 m), 750 mls (1 207 km) at 185 mph (298 km/h) at 12,500 ft (3 810 m); max. range (no reserves), 808 mls (1 300 km) at 3,000 ft (915 m); initial climb, 2,000 ft/min (10,16 m/sec); service ceiling, 20,010 ft (6 100 m).
Weights: Empty, 2,039 lb (925 kg); max. take-off (aerobatic), 2,977 lb (1 350 kg), (normal category), 3,483 lb (1 580 kg).
Status: First prototype (D1) flown on October 27, 1977 (with coupled Audi-NSU Wankel rotating piston engines), this being followed by the second prototype (D2) on May 31, 1978 (with Allison 250-C20B). First prototype re-engined with Allison turboshaft late 1978.
Notes: A highly original primary-basic trainer, the Fantrainer 400 utilises the integrated ducted-fan propulsion system and is of simple modular design of metal and glassfibre-reinforced plastic construction. It is claimed to reproduce some of the handling characteristics of high-performance combat aircraft and specific characteristics may be enhanced by the application of different wings, Rhein-Flugzeugbau currently proposing three interchangeable sets of wings.

RHEIN-FLUGZEUGBAU FANTRAINER 400

Dimensions: Span, 31 ft 6 in (9,60 m); length, 29 ft 4 in (8,95 m); height, 9 ft 6 in (2,90 m); wing area, 149·6 sq ft (13,90 m²).

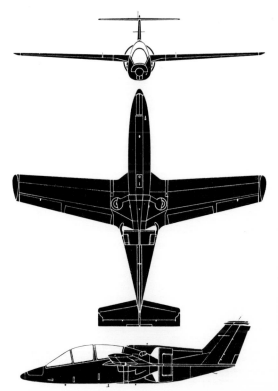

ROCKWELL SABRELINER 65

Country of Origin: USA.

Type: Light business executive transport.

Power Plant: Two 3,700 lb (1 678 kg) Garrett AiResearch TFE 731-3-1D turbofans.

Performance: Max. speed, 528 mph (850 km/h), or Mach 0·8; recommended cruise, 495 mph (796 km/h), or Mach 0·75; long-range cruise, 462 mph (743 km/h), or Mach 0·7; range (four passengers and VFR reserve), 3,328 mls (5 354 km); initial climb 4,950 ft/min (25,15 m/sec); cruise altitude, 39,000 ft (11 890 m).

Weights: Empty equipped, 13,350 lb (6 055 kg); max. take-off, 23,800 lb (10 795 kg).

Accommodation: Normal flight crew of two and basic cabin arrangements for seven, eight or ten passengers.

Status: First of three prototype Sabreliner 65s flown June 29, 1977 and first production aircraft on April 8, 1979 with seven delivered by beginning of 1980, when some 70 had been ordered.

Notes: The Sabreliner 65 is a progressive development of the Sabreliner 60 (see 1968 edition) with turbofans and utilising supercritical aerofoil technology, plain flaps being replaced by Fowler-type flaps, spoilers replacing the centreline air brake, an aft fuselage fuel tank being introduced and wing fuel capacity being increased.

ROCKWELL SABRELINER 65

Dimensions: Span, 50 ft $5\frac{1}{10}$ in (15,38 m); length, 46 ft 11 in (14,30 m); height, 16 ft 0 in (4,88 m); wing area, 380 sq ft (35,30 m²).

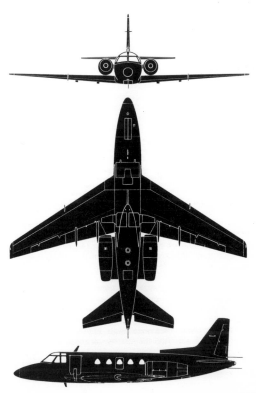

SAAB SAFARI TS

Country of Origin: Sweden.

Type: Three-seat primary-basic trainer and utility aircraft.

Power Plant: One 210 hp Continental TSIO-360 six-cylinder horizontally-opposed engine.

Performance: (At 2,205 lb/1 000 kg) Max. speed, 161 mph (260 km/h) at sea level; cruise (75% power), 140 mph (226 km/h) at sea level, 160 mph (257 km/h) at 12,000 ft (3 660 m); initial climb, 1,300 ft/min (6,6 m/sec); time to 12,000 ft (3 660 m), 9·5 min; service ceiling, 20,000 ft (6 095 m).

Weights: Max. take-off (aerobatic), 1,980 lb (900 kg), (utility), 2,480 lb (1 125 kg), (normal), 2,645 lb (1 200 kg).

Status: The Safari TS was announced mid-1979 as the latest model in the Safari/Supporter series of light aircraft, the prototype of which was flown (as the MFI 15) on July 11, 1969. By the beginning of 1980, production (all versions) totalled approximately 200 aircraft and suspended in 1978, was being resumed with the Safari TS.

Notes: The Safari TS is a turbo-supercharged version of the basic Safari intended primarily as a military trainer. The aircraft has six wing strong points and can carry up to 660 lb (300 kg) externally, allowing it to be used in such roles as coastal patrol (with up to six life rafts under the wings), reconnaissance with or without fixed camera installation, border patrol, light close support, etc. Previously, the military version of the Safari was known as the Supporter (this having been supplied to the Danish Air Force and Army and to the Pakistan Air Force), but both civil and military versions of the aircraft are now named Safari.

SAAB SAFARI TS

Dimensions: Span, 29 ft 0½ in (8,85 m); length, 22 ft 11½ in (7,00 m); height, 8 ft 6½ in (2,60 m); wing area, 128·1 sq ft (11,90 m²).

SAAB (JA) 37 VIGGEN

Country of Origin: Sweden.

Type: Single-seat all-weather intercepter fighter with secondary strike capability.

Power Plant: One 16,203 lb (7 350 kg) dry and 28,108 lb (12 750 kg) reheat Volvo Flygmotor RM 8B.

Performance: (Estimated) Max. speed (with two RB 24 Sidewinder AAMs), 1,320 mph (2 125 km/h) above 36,090 ft (11 000 m) or Mach 2·0, 910 mph (1 465 km/h) at 1,000 ft (305 m) or Mach 1·2; operational radius (M = 2·0 intercept with two AAMs), 250 mls (400 km), (LO-LO-LO ground attack with six Mk. 82 bombs), 300 mls (480 km); time (from brakes off) to 32,810 ft (10 000 m), 1·4 min.

Weights: (Estimated) Empty, 26,895 lb (12 200 kg); loaded (two AAMs), 37,040 lb (16 800 kg); max. take-off, 49,600 lb (22 500 kg).

Armament: One semi-externally mounted 30-mm Oerlikon KCA cannon with 150 rounds and up to 13,227 lb (6 000 kg) of ordnance on seven external stores stations.

Status: First of four JA 37 prototypes (modified from AJ 37 airframes) flown June 1974, with fifth prototype built from outset to JA 37 standards flown December 15, 1975. Initial production JA 37 flown on November 4, 1977. Total of 149 JA 37s (of 329 Viggens of all types) being procured.

Notes: The JA 37 is a development of the AJ 37 (see 1973 edition) which is optimised for the attack role. The JA 37 has uprated turbofan, will carry a mix of BAe Sky Flash AAMs and cannon armament, and has X-Band Pulse Doppler radar. The JA 37 attained initial operational capability in 1979, when a further attack development of this model was under consideration.

SAAB (JA) 37 VIGGEN

Dimensions: Span, 34 ft 9¼ in (10,60 m); length (excluding probe), 50 ft 8¼ in (15,45 m); height, 19 ft 4¼ in (5,90 m); wing area (including foreplanes), 561·88 sq ft (52,20 m²).

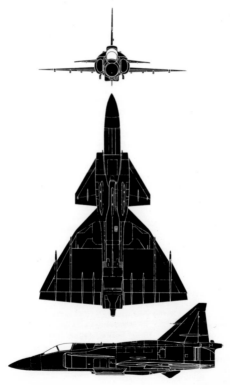

SEPECAT JAGUAR INTERNATIONAL

Countries of Origin: France and United Kingdom.
Type: Single-seat tactical strike fighter.
Power Plant: Two 5,320 lb (2 410 kg) dry and 8,040 lb (3 645 kg) reheat Rolls-Royce/Turboméca RT172-26 Adour 804, or 5,520 lb (2 504 kg) dry and 8,400 lb (3 811 kg) reheat RT172-58 Adour 811 turbofans.
Performance: (With -26 Adours and at typical weights) Max. speed, 820 mph (1 320 km/h) or Mach 1·1 at 1,000 ft (305 m), 1,057 mph (1 700 km/h) or Mach 1·6 at 32,810 ft (10 000 m); range (external fuel), 564 mls (907 km) LO-LO-LO, 875 mls (1 408 km) HI-LO-HI; ferry range, 2,190 mls (3 524 km).
Weights: Typical empty, 15,432 lb (7 000 kg); normal loaded, 24,000 lb (10 886 kg); max. take-off, 34,000 lb (15,422 lb).
Armament: Two 30-mm Aden or DEFA cannon and up to 10,000 lb (4 536 kg) ordnance on five external hardpoints. Provision for two AAMs (e.g., Matra 550 Magic) on overwing pylons.
Status: The Jaguar International is an export version of the basic Jaguar, the first of eight prototypes of which was flown on September 8,1968, 202 (including 37 two-seaters) having been delivered to the RAF and 176 (including 40 two-seaters) to the *Armée de l'Air*, 24 remaining to be delivered to the latter at the beginning of 1980. Twelve Jaguar Internationals have been delivered to both Ecuador and Oman in 1977 and 1977–78 respectively, and 40 (including five two-seaters) being scheduled for delivery to India 1981–82, with 100 plus being licence-built in that country from 1982.

SEPECAT JAGUAR INTERNATIONAL

Dimensions: Span, 28 ft 6 in (8,69 m); length, 50 ft 11 in (15,52 m); height, 16 ft 0½ in (4,89 m); wing area, 260·3 sq ft (24, 18 m²).

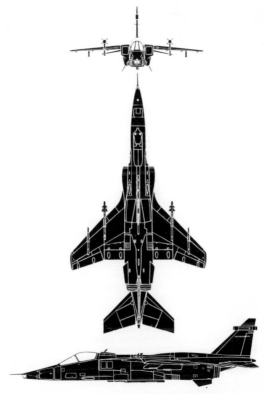

(SHENYANG) CHICHAO LIENCHI 6 (BT-6)

Country of Origin: Chinese Republic.

Type: Tandem two-seat primary trainer.

Power Plant: One 285 hp Jia Hou-sai 6 (AI-14R) nine-cylinder radial air-cooled engine.

Performance: Max. speed, 178 mph (286 km/h); initial climb, 1,248 ft/min (6,33 m/sec); service ceiling, 16,680 ft (5 085 m); endurance, 3·6 hrs.

Weights: Empty, 2,415 lb (1 095 kg); max. take-off, 3,088 lb (1 400 kg).

Status: The BT-6 entered production 1974—75 in succession to the licence-built Yak-18A (BT-5), some 2,000 examples of which were built, and the BT-6 has since been exported to Bangladesh, North Korea and Zambia.

Notes: The BT-6 (Type 6 Basic Training Aircraft, or *Chichao Lienchi Sinshi-liyu*), although similar in configuration to the Yak-18A, is, in fact, of original indigenous design and has largely replaced the licence-built Soviet trainer in service with the so-called Air Force of the People's Liberation Army. Development of the BT-6 was undertaken by the State Aircraft Factory at Shenyang, but series production is understood to be undertaken by another factory (either Beijing or Harbin), and the export of this trainer began in 1978, the most recent recipient being the air arm of Bangladesh which procured a number of BT-6s for primary-basic training at the newly-established Jessore flying school early in 1979.

(SHENYANG) CHICHAO LIENCHI 6 (BT-6)

Dimensions: Span, 35 ft 1¼ in (10,70 m); length, 27 ft 10¾ in (8,50 m); height, 10 ft 6 in (3,20 m).

(SHENYANG) CHAENCHI 6-ITSI
(F-6BIS FANTAN-A)

Country of Origin: Chinese Republic.

Type: Single-seat tactical strike fighter.

Power Plant: Two 5,730 lb (2 600 kg) and 7,165 lb (3 250 kg) Shenyang-built Tumanski RD-9B-811 turbojets.

Performance: (Estimated) Max. Speed, 900 mph (1 450 km/h) at 33,000 ft (10 000 m) or Mach 1·35; range cruise, 590 mph (950 km/h) or Mach 0·83; initial climb, 22,600 ft/min (115 m/sec); normal range, 860 mls (1 385 km); max. range (max. external fuel), 1,360 mls (2 190 km).

Weights: (Estimated) Empty, 13,000 lb (5 900 kg); normal loaded, 17,000 lb (7 700 kg); max. takeoff, 19,000 lb (8 620 kg).

Armament: Two 30-mm cannon in wing roots. Four wing stores stations for ordnance, two external fuselage stores stations and internal weapons bay.

Status: Known to have been built in some numbers by the State Aircraft Factories at Shenyang and Tientsin in the mid 'seventies, but present production status is unknown.

Notes: The F-6bis (Type 6bis Fighter, or *Sinshi-liyu-itsi Chaenchi*, but usually known simply as the *Kiangchi* (Attack Plane) and assigned the reporting name Fantan-A in the west, is a derivative of the Chinese-built MiG-19S, or F-6, evolved at Shenyang for the tactical strike role. It differs from the Soviet original primarily in having a redesigned forward fuselage with lateral air intakes, extended flaps and a bay in the lower portion of the fuselage, aft of the cockpit. Fitted with hinged doors, this bay is used to stow bombs and may also accommodate an auxiliary fuel tank. Several versions of the MiG-19 have been manufactured in China and production of the basic MiG-19S (*Chaenchi 6-bin*) was continuing at approximately 60 monthly at the beginning of 1980.

(SHENYANG) CHAENCHI 6-ITSI (KIANGCHI)

Dimensions: Span, 29 ft 6 in (9,00 m); length (without probe) 47 ft 0 in (14,30 m); height, 13 ft 0 in (3,95 m).

SHORTS 330

Country of Origin: United Kingdom.
Type: Third-level airliner and utility transport.
Power Plant: Two 1,173 shp Pratt & Whitney (Canada) PT6A-45A turboprops.
Performance: Max. cruise, 221 mph (356 km/h) at 10,000 ft (3 050 m); range cruise, 184 mph (296 km/h) at 10,000 ft; range (with 30 passengers and baggage, no reserve), 450 mls (725 km), (typical freighter configuration with 7,500-lb/ 3 400 kg payload), 368 mls (592 km); max range (passenger configuration with 4,060-lb/1 840-kg payload), 1,013 mls (1 630 km), (freighter configuration with 5,400-lb/2 450-kg payload), 1,013 mls (1 630 km); max. climb, 1,210 ft/min (6,14 m/sec).
Weights: Empty equipped (for 30 passengers), 14,500 lb (6 577 kg); max. take-off, 22,400 lb (10 160 kg).
Accommodation: Standard flight crew of two and normal accommodation for 30 passengers in 10 rows three abreast and 1,000 lb (455 kg) of baggage.
Status: Engineering prototype flown August 22, 1974, with production prototype following on July 8, 1975. First production aircraft flown on December 15, 1975. Customer deliveries commenced mid-1976, and at the beginning of 1980 a total of 43 aircraft had been ordered with approximately 36 delivered.
Notes: The Shorts 330 is derived from the Skyvan STOL utility transport (see 1975 edition) and is designed primarily for commuter and regional air service operators. Retaining many of the Skyvan's characteristics, including its large cabin cross section, Shorts 330 had been ordered by 13 operators by the beginning of 1980.

SHORTS 330

Dimensions: Span, 74 ft 8 in (22,76 m); length, 58 ft 0½ in (17,69 m); height, 16 ft 3 in (4,95 m); wing area, 453 sq ft (42,10 m²).

SIAI MARCHETTI SF-600 CANGURO

Country of Origin: Italy.

Type: Light utility transport.

Power Plant: Two 350 hp Avco Lycoming TIO-540-J six-cylinder horizontally-opposed engines.

Performance: Max. speed, 212 mph (340 km/h) at 15,000 ft (4 575 m); cruise (60% power), 168 mph (270 km/h) at 12,000 ft (3 655 m); initial climb, 1,350 ft/min (6,85 m/sec); max. ceiling, 23,280 ft (7 100 m); range (with 1,985 lb/900 kg), 310 mls (500 km), (with 1,100 lb/500 kg), 995 mls (1 600 km).

Weights: Empty equipped (freighter), 4,295 lb (1 950 kg); max. take-off, 6,828 lb (3 100 kg).

Accommodation: Crew of one or two and up to 10 passengers or four stretcher patients and two medical attendants in main cabin.

Status: Prototype SF-600 (built by Costruzioni Aeronautiche General Avia) flown late December 1978, marketing and future production being in the hands of the Siai Marchetti concern.

Notes: Of generally similar concept to the Pilatus Britten-Norman Islander (see pages 176–177), the Canguro (Kangaroo) has been designed to take either piston engines (as above) or turboprops, and the prototype is to be converted to take 400 shp Allison 250B-17 turboprops for comparative trials. The anticipated performance with turboprops is generally similar to that of the piston-engined model, apart from maximum and cruise speeds which are estimated at 224 mph (361 km/h) at 15,000 ft (4 575 m) and 193 mph (311 km/h) at 12,000 ft (3 655 m) respectively. A production decision had not been taken at the time of closing for press.

SIAI MARCHETTI SF-600 CANGURO

Dimensions: Span, 47 ft 6½ in (14,50 m); length, 39 ft 10 in (12,15 m); height, 15 ft 1 in (4,60 m); wing area, 248·7 sq ft (23,10 m²).

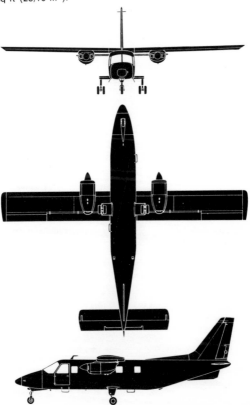

SUKHOI SU-17 (FITTER-D)

Country of Origin: USSR.
Type: Single-seat tactical strike fighter.
Power Plant: One 17,195 lb (7 800 kg) dry and 24,700 lb (11 200 kg) reheat Lyulka AL-21F-3 turbojet.
Performance: Max. speed (clean), 808 mph (1 300 km/h) or Mach 1·06 at sea level, 1,430 mph (2 300 km/h) at 39,370 ft (12 000 m) or Mach 2·17; combat radius (lo-lo-lo mission profile), 260 mls (420 km), (hi-lo-hi mission profile), 373 mls (600 km); range (with 2,205-lb/1 000-kg weapon load and auxiliary fuel), 1,415 mls (2 280 km); service ceiling, 57,415 ft (17 500 m).
Weights: Max. take-off, 39,022 lb (17 700 kg).
Armament: Two 30-mm NR-30 cannon with 70 rpg and (for short-range missions) a max. external ordnance load of 7,716 lb (3 500 kg)
Status: A derivative of the Su-7, the Su-17 entered service with the Soviet Air Forces in 1972 (in Fitter-C form), having since been exported (with varying equipment standards as the Su-20 and Su-22) to Algeria, Czechoslovakia, Egypt, Iraq, Libya, Peru, Poland, South Yemen and Syria.
Notes: The Fitter-D version of the Su-17, which appeared in 1976, features a lengthened nose beneath which is attached a flat fairing of elongated lozenge shape, the purpose of which had not been positively identified at the time of closing for press.

SUKHOI SU-17 (FITTER-D)

Estimated Dimensions: Span (max.), 45 ft 0 in (13,70 m), (min.), 32 ft 6 in (9,90 m); length (including probe) 58 ft 3 in (17,75 m); height, 15 ft 5 in (4,70 m).

SUKHOI SU-19 (FENCER-A)

Country of Origin: USSR.

Type: Two-seat ground attack fighter.

Power Plant: Two 17,635 lb (8 000 kg) dry and 25,350 lb (11 500 kg) reheat Tumansky R-29B turbofans.

Performance: (Estimated) Max. speed, 760–840 mph (1 225–1 350 km/h) at sea level or Mach 1·0–1·1, 1,385–1,520 mph (2 230–2 445 km/h) at 36,090 ft (11 000 m) or Mach 2·1–2·3; radius of action (lo-lo-lo), 250 mls (400 km), (hi-lo-hi), 750 mls (1 200 km); max. endurance, 3–4 hrs.

Weights: (Estimated) Empty equipped, 33,000 lb (14 970 kg); max. take-off, 68,000 lb (30 845 kg).

Armament: One six-barrel 23-mm rotary cannon in the underside of the fuselage and up to 10,000–11,000 lb (4 500–5 000 kg) of ordnance on six external stations (two under the fuselage and four under the fixed wing glove), a typical ordnance load comprising two 1,100-lb (500-kg) bombs, two surface-to-air missiles and two pods each containing 16 or 32 57-mm unguided rockets.

Status: Prototypes of the Su-19 are believed to have flown in 1970, and this type was first reported to be in service with the Soviet Air Forces during the course of 1974. Western intelligence agencies indicated that several hundred had attained service by the beginning of 1980.

Notes: The Su-19 (the accompanying illustrations of which should be considered as provisional) is the first Soviet fighter optimised for the ground attack role to have achieved service status. Wing leading-edge sweep varies from approximately 23 deg fully spread to 70 deg fully swept, and the wings reportedly incorporate both leading- and trailing-edge lift devices and lift dumpers acting as spoilers in conjunction with differential tail-plane movement for roll control.

SUKHOI SU-19 (FENCER-A)

Dimensions: (Estimated) Span (max.), 56 ft 0 in (17,00 m), (min.), 31 ft 0 in (9,45 m); length, 70 ft 0 in (21,25 m); height, 18 ft 0 in (5,50 m); wing area, 409 sq ft (38,00 m²).

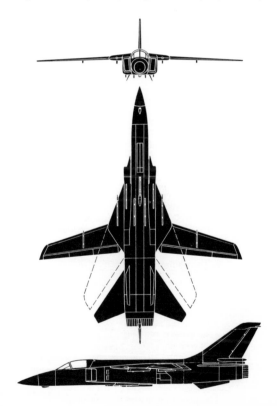

TRANSALL C.160

Countries of Origin: France and Federal Germany.

Type: Medium-range tactical transport.

Power Plant: Two 6,100 ehp Rolls-Royce Tyne RTy 20 Mk. 22 turboprops.

Performance: (At 112,435 lb/51 000 kg) Max. speed, 322 mph (518 km/h) at 16,000 ft (4 875 m); econ. cruise, 282 mph (454 km/h) at 20,000 ft (6 100 m); range (with 35,274-lb/ 16 000-kg payload), 783 mls (1 260 km), (with 17,640-lb/ 8 000-kg payload), 2,734 mls (4 400 km), (with 6,614-lb/ 3 000-kg payload), 4,350 mls (7 000 km); ferry range, 5,500 mls (8 850 km); max. initial climb, 1,300 ft/min (6,6 m/sec).

Weights: Basic operational 63,814 lb (28 946 kg); max. take-off, 108,245 lb (49 100 kg).

Accommodation: Crew of three and 62–88 paratroops, max. of 93 fully-equipped troops, up to 63 casualty stretchers and four medical attendants, or loads up to 37,500 lb (17 000 kg).

Status: First prototype flown February 25, 1963, and two further prototypes and 179 production aircraft built by time series manufacture terminated in 1972. Production resumed in 1978 against requirement for further 25 aircraft for *Armée de l'Air* and three for *Postale de Nuit,* with deliveries to commence 1981. Production being shared equally between France (Aéro-spatiale) and Germany (MBB and VFW). Three C.160s were ordered in 1979 by the Indonesian government.

Notes: The new series C.160 embodies a number of modifica-tions. The flight crew complement has been reduced from four to three, the wing centre section now contains 1,980 Imp gal (9 000 l) of fuel, flight refuelling equipment is provided and the aircraft can also operate as a flight refuelling tanker, a new autopilot system has been introduced and the forward fuselage has been redesigned to eliminate the port freight door.

TRANSALL C-160

Dimensions: Span, 131 ft 3 in (40,00 m); length, 106 ft 4 in (32,40 m); height, 38 ft 3 in (11,65 m); wing area, 1,723·3 sq ft (160,10 m²).

TUPOLEV BACKFIRE-B

Country of Origin: USSR.

Type: Long-range strike and maritime recce-strike aircraft.

Power Plant: Two (estimated) 33,070 lb (15 000 kg) dry and 46,300 lb (21 000 kg) reheat Kuznetsov turbofans.

Performance: (Estimated) Max. (short-period) speed, 1,320 mph (2 125 km/h) at 39,370 ft (12 000 m) or Mach 2·0; max. sustained speed, 1,190 mph (1 915 km/h) at 39,370 ft (12 000 m) or Mach 1·8, 685 mph (1 100 km/h) at sea level or Mach 0·9; cruise, 495 mph (795 km/h) at sea level or Mach 0·65, 530 mph (850 km/h) at 39,370 ft (12 000 m) or Mach 0·8; unrefuelled combat radius (including 400 mls/250 km at Mach 1·8), 2,485 mls (4 000 km) for HI-LO-HI (200 mls/320 km at low altitude) profile.

Weights: (Estimated) Operational empty, 114,640 lb (52 000 kg); max. take-off, 260,000 lb (118 000 kg).

Armament: One or two externally-mounted AS-6 Kingfish 340-mile (740-km) range inertially-guided stand-off missiles or internal weapons load of approx. 15,000 lb (6 800 kg). Remotely-controlled 23-mm cannon tail barbette.

Status: Reported in prototype form in 1969, the Backfire apparently began to enter service with both the long-range element of the SovAF and the Soviet naval air arm in 1974, with combined total of 150–160 in service at the beginning of 1980, when production rate was estimated at 2·5 monthly. There is some confusion as to the correct designation of this type, Soviet sources referring to Tu-22M and western intelligence sources referring to Tu-26.

TUPOLEV BACKFIRE-B

Dimensions: (Estimated) Span (max.), 115 ft 0 in (35,00 m), (min.), 92 ft 0 in (28,00 m); length, 138 ft 0 in (42,00 m); height, 29 ft 6 in (9,00 m); wing area, 1,830 sq ft (170 m²).

TUPOLEV TU-154B (CARELESS)

Country of Origin: USSR.

Type: Medium- to long-haul commercial transport.

Power Plant: Three 23,150 lb (10 500 kg) Kuznetsov NK-8-2U turbofans.

Performance: Max. cruise, 590 mph (950 km/h) at 31,000 ft (9 450 m); econ. cruise, 559 mph (900 km/h) at 36,090 ft (11 000 m); range (with max. payload—39,683 lb), 1,710 mls (2 750 km), (with 160 passengers), 2,020 mls (3 250 km), (with 120 passengers), 2,485 mls (4 000 km).

Weights: Max. take-off, 211,644 lb (96 000 kg).

Accommodation: Crew of three on flight-deck and basic arrangements for 160 single-class passengers in six-abreast seating, eight first-class and 150 tourist-class passengers, or (high density) 169 passengers.

Status: Prototype Tu-154 flown on October 4, 1968, current production model being the Tu-154B (introduced by Aeroflot in 1976) of which approximately four per month were being manufactured at the beginning of 1980. More than 320 Tu-154s (all versions) are currently in service with Aeroflot and the Tu-154B has also been supplied to Malev (three) of Hungary.

Notes: The Tu-154B combines the improvements introduced by the Tu-154A with major changes in controls and systems, and slight increases in weights. The wing spoilers have been extended in span and are now used for low-speed lateral control and passenger capacity has been increased by extending the usable cabin area rearwards, and an extra emergency exit has been added on each side of the fuselage. Various longer-range versions of the basic Tu-154 are known to be under study, including one reportedly powered by NK-86 turbofans similar to those of the Il-86.

TUPOLEV TU-154B (CARELESS)

Dimensions: Span, 123 ft $2\frac{1}{2}$ in (37,55 m); length, 157 ft $1\frac{3}{4}$ in (47,90 m); height, 37 ft $4\frac{3}{4}$ in (11,40 m); wing area, 2,168·92 sq ft (201,45 m²).

VALMET L-70 MILTRAINER

Country of Origin: Finland.

Type: Side-by-side two-seat primary trainer.

Power Plant: One 200 hp Avco Lycoming AEIO-360-A1B6 four-cylinder horizontally-opposed engine.

Performance: Max. speed (at 2,204 lb/1 000 kg), 149 mph (240 km/h) at sea level, (at max. take-off weight), 143 mph (230 km/h); cruise (75% power), 130 mph (210 km/h) at sea level; initial climb, 1,122 ft/min (5,7 m/sec); service ceiling, 15,090 ft (4 600 m); range (max. pay-load and no reserves), 534 mls (860 km).

Weights: Empty equipped, 1,691 lb (767 kg); max. take-off (aerobatic), 2,293 lb (1 040 kg), (normal category), 2,756 lb (1 250 kg).

Status: L-70X prototype flown July 1, 1975, and first production aircraft was scheduled to fly November 1979, with initial deliveries against order for 30 for Finnish Air Force commencing second quarter of 1980.

Notes: Assigned the name Vinka (Blast) by the Finnish Air Force, the Miltrainer is to replace the Saab Safir as the service's primary-basic trainer. Four hardpoints in the wings can lift external loads up to 660 lb (300 kg), suiting the Miltrainer for armament training or, when flown as a single-seater, the tactical support mission.

VALMET L-70 MILTRAINER

Dimensions: Span, 32 ft 3¾ in (9,85 m); length, 24 ft 7¼ in (7,50 m); height, 10 ft 0⅓ in (3,31 m); wing area, 150·69 sq ft (14,00 m²).

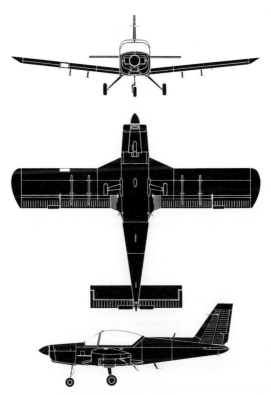

VOUGHT A-7K CORSAIR II

Country of Origin: USA.

Type: Tandem two-seat tactical strike fighter and operational proficiency aircraft.

Power Plant: One 15,000 lb (6 804 kg) Allison TF41-A-2 (Rolls-Royce Spey) turbofan.

Performance: Max. speed, 690 mph (1 110 km/h) at sea level; 685 mph (1 102 km/h) at 5,000 ft (1 525 m), (with 12 Mk. 82 bombs), 646 mph (1 040 km/h) at 5,000 ft (1 525 m); combat range (with eight 800-lb/363-kg M117 bombs and two 250 Imp gal/1 136 1 drop tanks), 1,340 mls (2 156 km) at average cruise of 508 mph (817 km/h); initial climb (at 42,000 lb/19 050 kg), 10,900 ft/min (55,3 m/sec).

Weights: Basic empty, 20,800 lb (9 435 kg); max. take-off, 42,000 lb (19 050 kg).

Armament: One 20-mm M61A-1 Vulcan rotary cannon in port side of fuselage and up to 14,000 lb (6 350 kg) of ordnance on eight (two fuselage and six wing) external stations.

Status: One prototype A-7K converted from A-7D airframe was scheduled to fly late 1979, with initial batch of 12 new-build aircraft (for Air National Guard) for delivery second half of 1980.

Notes: The A-7K is essentially a two-seat derivative of the single-seat A-7D with a similar 34-in (86,4-cm) fuselage plug (to accommodate the second cockpit) and marginally larger vertical tail surfaces to those of the US Navy's TA-7C (converted from A-7B and A-7C airframes with a Pratt & Whitney TF30-P-408 turbofan) and the Hellenic Air Force's TA-7H (similarly powered to the A-7K), the latter being a new-build two-seat version of the A-7H, which, in turn, is a Greek version of the A-7D.

VOUGHT A-7K CORSAIR II

Dimensions: Span, 38 ft 8¾ in (11,80 m); length, 48 ft 8 in (14,80 m); height, 16 ft 3⅜ in (4,97 m); wing area, 375 sq ft (34,83 m²).

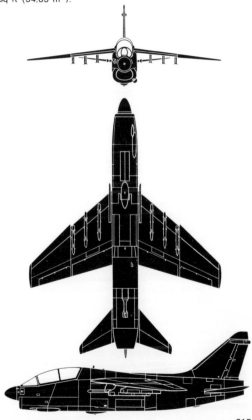

YAKOVLEV YAK-36MP (FORGER-A)

Country of Origin: USSR.
Type: Single-seat shipboard air defence and strike fighter.
Power Plant: One (approx.) 17,640 lb (8 000 kg) lift/cruise turbojet plus two 7,935 lb (3 600 kg) lift turbojets.
Performance: (Estimated) Max. speed, 695 mph (1 120 km/h) above 36,000 ft (10 970 m), or Mach 1·05, 725 mph (1 167 km/h) at sea level, or Mach 0·95; high-speed cruise, 595 mph (958 km/h) at 20,000 ft (6 095 m), or Mach 0·85; combat radius (internal fuel and 2,205-lb/1 000-kg external ordnance), 230 mls (370 km), (with two 110 Imp gal/500 l drop tanks, a reconnaissance pod and two AAMs), 340 mls (547 km); initial climb, 20,000 ft/min (101,6 m/sec).
Weights: (Estimated) Empty, 12,125 lb (5 500 kg); max. take-off, 22,000 lb (9 980 kg).
Armament: Four underwing pylons with total capacity of (approx.) 2,205 lb (1 000 kg), including twin-barrel 23-mm cannon pods, air-to-air missiles or bombs.
Status: The Yak-36MP (Forger-A) is believed to have flown in prototype form in 1971 and to have attained service evaluation status in 1976 aboard the carriers *Kiev* and *Minsk*.
Notes: Possessing no short-landing-and-take-off (STOL) capability, being limited to vertical-take-off-and-landing (VTOL operation), the Yak-36 combines a vectored-thrust lift/cruise engine with fore and aft lift engines. The single-seat Yak-36MP possesses no attack radar and no internal armament. A tandem two-seat version, the Yak-36UV (Forger-B), has an extended forward fuselage. A second seat is added ahead of that of the Yak-36MP and the nose is drooped to provide a measure of vertical stagger and the aft fuselage is also extended in order to maintain the CG. The two-seat conversion training version is illustrated above.

YAKOVLEV YAK-36MP (FORGER-A)

Dimensions: (Estimated) Span, 24 ft 7 in (7,50 m); length, 52 ft 6 in (16,00 m); height, 11 ft 0 in (3,35 m); wing area, 167 sq ft (15,50 m²).

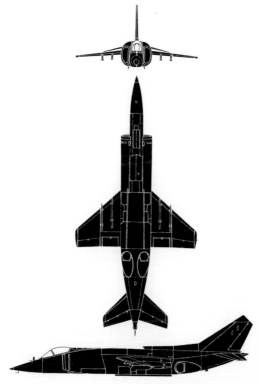

YAKOVLEV YAK-42 (CLOBBER)

Country of Origin: USSR.

Type: Short- to medium-haul commercial transport.

Power Plant: Three 14,320 lb (6 500 kg) Lotarev D-36 turbofans.

Performance: Econ. cruise, 510 mph (820 km/h) at 25,000 ft (7 600 m): range (max. payload—31,938 lb/14 500 kg), 620 mls (1 000 km), (with 26,430-lb/12 000-kg payload), 1,150 mls (1 850 km); max. range, 1,520 mls (2 450 km); time to cruise altitude (25,000 ft/7 600 m), 11 min.

Weights: Operational empty, 63,845 lb (28 960 kg); max. take-off, 114,640 lb (52 000 kg).

Accommodation: Basic flight crew of two and various alternative cabin arrangements, including 76 passengers in a mixed-class layout (16 first class), 100 passengers in a single-class layout with six-abreast seating and 120 passengers in a high-density layout.

Status: First prototype flown on March 7, 1975, followed by second in April 1976. A production prototype was flown in February 1977, and deliveries to Aeroflot were scheduled to commence during 1979.

Notes: The initial prototypes of the Yak-42 differed one from the other in wing sweep angle, the first prototype featuring 11 deg of sweepback and the second 25 deg, the latter sweep angle being adopted for production aircraft. The Yak-42 is intended for operation primarily over relatively short stages and utilising restricted airfields with poor surfaces and limited facilities in the remoter areas of the Soviet Union. Independent of airport ground equipment and having a heavy-duty undercarriage, the Yak-42 bears a resemblance to the Yak-40.

YAKOVLEV YAK-42 (CLOBBER)

Dimensions: Span, 112 ft 2½ in (34,20 m); length, 119 ft 4 in (36,38 m); height, 32 ft 3 in (9,83 m); wing area, 1,615 sq ft (150,00 m²).

AÉROSPATIALE SA 330J PUMA

Country of Origin: France.
Type: Medium transport helicopter.
Power Plant: Two 1,575 shp Turboméca IVC turboshafts.
Performance: Max. speed, 163 mph (262 km/h); max. continuous cruise at sea level, 159 mph (257 km/h); max. inclined climb, 1,400 ft/min (7,1 m/sec); hovering ceiling (in ground effect), 7,315 ft (2 230 m), (out of ground effect), 4,430 ft (1 350 m); max. range (standard fuel), 342 mls (550 km).
Weights: Empty, 7,969 lb (3 615 kg); max. take-off 16,534 lb (7 500 kg).
Dimensions: Rotor diam, 49 ft 5¾ in (15,08 m); fuselage length, 46 ft 1½ in (14,06 m).
Notes: The civil SA 330J and the equivalent military SA 330L (illustrated) were the current production models of the Puma at the beginning of 1980 when more than 650 Pumas of all versions had been ordered. The SA 330J and 330L differ from the civil SA 330F (passenger) and SA 330G (cargo), and SA 330H (military) models that immediately preceded them in having new plastic blades accompanied by increases in gross weights. The SA 330B (French Army), SA 330C (export) and SA 330E (RAF) had 1,328 shp Turmo IIIC4 turboshafts. Components for the Puma are supplied by Westland in the UK (representing approx. 15% of the airframe) and production was 5–7 Pumas monthly at the beginning of 1980. The Puma has been delivered to some 45 countries.

AÉROSPATIALE AS 332 SUPER PUMA

Country of Origin: France.
Type: Medium transport helicopter (21 seats).
Power Plant: Two 1,780 shp Turboméca Makila 1 turbo-shafts.
Performance: Max. cruising speed, 181 mph (291 km/h); econ. cruise, 161 mph (260 km/h); hovering ceiling (in ground effect), 9,840 ft (3 000 m), (out of ground effect), 7,545 ft (2 300 m); range, 564 mls (908 km) at sea level.
Weights: Empty, 8,443 lb (3 830 kg); max. take-off, 17,196 lb (7 800 kg).
Dimensions: Rotor diam, 49 ft 5¾ in (15,08 m); fuselage length, 46 ft 1½ in (14,06 m).
Notes: The definitive version of the upgraded SA 330 Puma (see opposite page), the AS 332 Super Puma differs primarily in having a twin-Makila power plant with uprated and simpli-fied transmission, composite rotor blades and new avionics. The first production standard SA 332 prototype was flown on September 13, 1978, being preceded on September 5, 1977 by the Makila-powered AS 331 test-bed, and production deliv-eries are scheduled to commence late 1980, civil and military versions being marketed in parallel. The military version (AS 332B) can accommodate 16 fully-equipped troops or, in the aeromedical role, six stretcher casualties and seven seated casualties. Orders for the RAF and the French Army were being negotiated late 1979.

AÉROSPATIALE SA 342 GAZELLE

Country of Origin: France.
Type: Five-seat light utility helicopter.
Power Plant: One 870 shp Turboméca Astazou XIVM turbo-shaft.
Performance: Max. speed, 193 mph (310 km/h); max. continuous cruise at sea level, 168 mph (270 km/h); max. inclined climb, 2,066 ft/min (10,5 m/sec); hovering ceiling (in ground effect), 13,120 ft (4 000 m), (out of ground effect), 10,330 ft (3 150 m); range at sea level, 488 mls (785 km).
Weights: Empty equipped, 2,149 lb (975 kg); max. take-off, 4,190 lb (1 900 kg).
Dimensions: Rotor diam, 34 ft 5½ in (10,50 m); fuselage length, 31 ft 2¾ in (9,53 m).
Notes: The SA 342 is a more powerful derivative of the SA 341 (592 shp Astazou IIIA) and has been exported to Kuwait, Iraq and elsewhere, and is equipped to launch four HOT missiles, AS-11s or other weapons. A civil equivalent, the SA 342J offering a 220 lb (100 kg) increase in payload, became available in 1977, and sales of the SA 341 and 342 Gazelles totalled some 850 by the beginning of 1980. Versions of the lower-powered SA 341 comprise the SA 341B (British Army), SA 341C (British Navy), SA 341D (RAF), SA 341F (French Army), SA 341G (civil version) and SA 341H (military export version). The latest military version is the SA 342M with a six-HOT installation for delivery to the French Army from 1980, 160 having been ordered.

AÉROSPATIALE AS 350 ECUREUIL

Country of Origin: France.

Type Six-seat light general-purpose utility helicopter.

Power Plant: One (AS 350B) 641 shp Turboméca Arriel or (AS 350D) 615 shp Avco Lycoming LTS 101-600A2 turbo-shaft.

Performance: Max. speed, 169 mph (272 km/h) at sea level; cruise, 144 mph (232 km/h) at sea level; max. climb, 1,810 ft/min (9,2 m/sec); hovering ceiling (in ground effect), 9,678 ft (2 950 m), (out of ground effect), 7,382 ft (2 250 m); range, 435 mls (700 km) at sea level.

Weights: Empty, 2,304 lb (1 045 kg); max. take-off, 4,299 lb (1 950 kg).

Dimensions: Rotor diam. 35 ft 0¾ in (10,69 m); fuselage length, 35 ft 9½ in (10,91 m).

Notes: First (LTS 101-powered) Ecureuil (Squirrel) Prototype flown on June 27, 1974, with second (Arriel-powered) follow-ing February 14, 1975. The Ecureuil is being manufactured with both types of power plant, the LTS 101-powered AS 350D being marketed in the USA as the AStar, some 400 having been ordered by North American customers by the beginning of 1980, when total orders for both versions exceeded 500 and production rate was building up to 23 monthly. The standard model is a six-seater and features include a Starflex all-platic rotor head, simplified dynamic machinery and modular assemblies to simplify changes in the field. Some 160 AS 350s had been delivered by the beginning of 1980.

AÉROSPATIALE AS 355E ECUREUIL 2

Country of Origin: France.
Type: Six-seat light general-purpose utility helicopter.
Power Plant: Two 425 shp Allison 250-C20F turboshafts.
Performance: Max. speed, 169 mph (272 km/h) at sea level; cruise, 149 mph (240 km/h) at sea level; max. climb, 1,710 ft/min (8,7 m/sec); hovering ceiling (in ground effect), 7,210 ft (2 200 m), (out of ground effect), 4,920 ft (1 500 m); range, 497 mls (800 km) at sea level.
Weights: Empty, 2,711 lb (1 230 kg); max. take-off, 4,630 lb (2 100 kg).
Dimensions: Rotor diam. 35 ft 0¾ in (10,69 m); fuselage length, 35 ft 9½ in (10,91 m).
Notes: Flown for the first time on September 27, 1979, the AS 355E Ecureuil 2 is a twin-engined derivative of the AS 350 (see page 223) intended primarily for the North American market on which it is marketed as the TwinStar. Claimed to be the cheapest and most compact twin-turboshaft helicopter available, more than 200 helicopters of this type had been ordered by customers in 10 countries by the beginning of 1980, when production schedules called for the commencement of deliveries in January 1981. The AS 355E Ecureuil 2 employs an essentially similar airframe and similar dynamic components to those of the AS 350 Ecureuil 1, including the composite material Starflex rotor head. Military versions are currently under development.

AÉROSPATIALE SA 361H DAUPHIN

Country of Origin: France.
Type: Light anti-armour helicopter.
Power Plant: One 1,400 shp Turboméca Astazou XXB turboshaft.
Performance: Max. cruising speed, 180 mph (289 km/h) at sea level, econ. cruise, 168 mph (270 km/h); max. climb, 2,885 ft/min (14,5 m/sec); hovering ceiling (in ground effect), 12,630 ft (3 850 m); range, 350 mls (565 km).
Weights: Max. take-off, 7,496 lb (3 400 kg).
Dimensions: Rotor diam, 38 ft 4 in (11,68 m); fuselage length, 40 ft 3 in (12,27 m).
Notes: The SA 361H/HCL (*hélicoptère de combat léger*) is an anti-armour version of the basic SA 361H military version of the Dauphin (its civil equivalent being the SA 361F). It is equipped with a forward-looking infra-red aiming system and up to eight HOT (High-subsonic Optically-guided Tube-launched) anti-armour missiles, but retains its capability to transport up to 13 fully-equipped troops. The first prototype Dauphin flew on June 2, 1972, production being initiated as the SA 360, and the prototype of the SA 361, an overpowered version intended specifically for hot-and-high operating conditions, followed on July 12, 1976. If ordered, the HCL model can be delivered in 1982. The SA 360 Dauphin is powered by a 1,050 shp Astazou XVIIIA and normally carries a pilot and nine passengers.

225

AÉROSPATIALE SA 365N DAUPHIN 2

Country of Origin: France.
Type: Multi-purpose and transport helicopter.
Power Plant: Two 701 shp Turbomeca Arriel 1C turboshafts.
Performance: Max. speed, 196 mph (315 km/h) at sea level; cruise, 169 mph (272 km/h) at sea level; max. climb, 1,692 ft/min (8,6 m/sec); hovering ceiling (in ground effect), 6,070 (1 850 m), (out of ground effect), 3,445 ft (1 050 m) range, 525 mls (845 km) at sea level.
Weights: Empty, 4,162 lb (1 888 kg); max. take-off, 7,935 lb (3 600 kg).
Dimensions: Rotor diam, 38 ft 3$\frac{1}{2}$ in (11,68 m); fuselage length, 37 ft 4 in (11,38 m).
Notes: The SA 365N, the prototype of which flew on March 31, 1979, is the latest variant of the Dauphin 2 and is intended to supplant the SA 365C (see 1979 edition) in production with deliveries commencing in the first half of 1981. The SA 366G powered by Avco Lycoming LTS 101-750 turboshafts is a version selected by the US Coast Guard which plans procurement of 90 from 1982 onwards, and a combined production rate (SA 365N and SA 366G) of 10–15 monthly is anticipated for 1982, with 19 SA 365Ns delivered by the end of 1981. Accommodating a pilot and up to 13 passengers, the SA 365N differs from the SA 365C in having uprated Arriel engines, a reprofiled fuselage, a fully-retractable undercarriage and increased fuel capacity in new under-floor tankage.

AGUSTA A 109A

Country of Origin: Italy.
Type: Eight-seat light utility helicopter.
Power Plant: Two 420 shp Allison 250-C20B turboshafts.
Performance: (At 5,402 lb/2 450 kg) Max. speed, 192 mph (310 km/h); max. continuous cruise, 173 mph (278 km/h) at sea level; hovering ceiling (in ground effect), 9,800 ft (2 987 m), (out of ground effect), 6,700 ft (2 042 m); max. inclined climb, 1,600 ft/min (8,12 m/sec); max. range, 385 mls (620 km) at 148 mph (238 km/h).
Weights: Empty equipped, 2,998 lb (1 360 kg); max. take-off, 5,780 lb (2 622 kg).
Dimensions: Rotor diam, 36 ft 1 in (11,00 m); fuselage length, 35 ft 2½ in (10,73 m).
Notes: The first of four A 109A prototypes flew on August 4, 1971. A pre-production batch of 10 A 109As was followed by first customer deliveries late 1976 with nearly 90 delivered by beginning of 1980, when production was running at seven machines monthly. The A109A is currently being offered for civil and military roles, five having been delivered to the Italian Army, including two equipped to launch TOW (Tube-launched Optically-tracked Wire-guided) missiles. Variants include a naval A 109A with search radar, gyro-stabilised weapons aiming sight and torpedo or rocket armament, and an electronic warfare version with active electronic counter-measures and passive electronic suppression equipment.

227

AGUSTA A 129 MANGUSTA

Country of Origin: Italy.

Type: Two-seat light attack helicopter.

Power Plant: Two 880 shp Avco Lycoming LTS-850A-1 turboshafts.

Performance: (Estimated) Max. speed. 177 mph (285 km/h) at sea level; cruise, 155 mph (250 km/h); max. climb, 1,968 ft/min (10 m/sec); hovering ceiling (in ground effect), 11,155 ft (3 400 m), (out of ground effect), 8,530 ft (2 600 m); endurance, 2·5 hrs (plus 20 min reserves).

Weights: Empty equipped, 4,976 lb (2 257 kg); max. take-off, 7,385 lb (3 350 kg).

Dimensions: Rotor diam, 39 ft 0½ in (11,90 m); fuselage length, 39 ft 10¾ in (12,16 m).

Notes: The A 129 Mangusta (Mongoose) is a dedicated light attack and anti-armour helicopter utilising some of the dynamic components of the A 109A (see page 227). Three prototypes of the A 129 are being built and the first of these is scheduled to commence its test programme late 1980. The Italian Army envisages an initial requirement for 60 A 129s with deliveries commencing 1982–3. The A 129 can carry eight TOW missiles plus two 7,62-mm gun pods or two 7×2·75-in rocket pods, eight Hellfire missiles with nose-mounted target acquisition and designation system and various other weapons systems. The A 129 possesses a very small cross section, and is claimed to offer low IR signature and exceptional agility.

AGUSTA-BELL AB 212ASW

Country of Origin: Italy.
Type: Anti-submarine and anti-surface vessel helicopter.
Power Plant: One 1,290 shp (derated from 1,875 shp) Pratt & Whitney PT6T-6 coupled turboshaft.
Performance: (At 11,197 lb/5 080 kg) Max. speed, 122 mph (196 km/h) at sea level; max. cruise, 115 mph (185 km/h); max. inclined climb, 1,450 ft/min (7,38 m/sec); hovering ceiling (in ground effect), 12,500 ft (3 810 m), (out of ground effect), 4,000 ft (1,220 m); range (15% reserves), 414 mls (667 km) at sea level.
Weights: Empty equipped, 7,540 lb (3 420 kg); max. take-off, 11,197 lb (5 080 kg).
Dimensions: Rotor diam, 48 ft $2\frac{1}{2}$ in (14,69 m); fuselage length, 42 ft $10\frac{3}{4}$ in (13,07 m).
Notes: The AB 212ASW is an Italian anti-submarine derivative of the Bell 212 Twin Two-Twelve (see page 230) developed primarily for use by the Italian Navy (to which 28 examples are being delivered) and for export (batches having been delivered to Peru, Spain and Turkey). For the ASW mission, the AB 212ASW carries high-performance long-range search radar, ECM equipment, a gyro-stabilised sighting system and a pair of Mk 44 or Mk 46 homing torpedoes or depth charges. Agusta also manufactures the standard AB 212 and the AB 205 Iroquois, combined production rate being 12—15 monthly at the beginning of 1980.

BELL MODEL 206B JETRANGER III

Country of Origin: USA.
Type: Five-seat light utility helicopter.
Power Plant: One 420 shp Allison 250-C20B turboshaft.
Performance: (At 3,200 lb/1 451 kg) Max. speed, 140 mph (225 km/h) at sea level; max. cruise, 133 mph (214 km/h) at sea level; hovering ceiling (in ground effect), 12,700 ft (3 871 m), (out of ground effect), 6,000 ft (1 829 m); max. range (no reserve), 360 mls (579, km).
Weights: Empty, 1,500 lb (680 kg); max. take-off, 3,200 lb (1 451 kg).
Dimensions: Rotor diam, 33 ft 4 in (10,16 m); fuselage length, 31 ft 2 in (9,50 m).
Notes: Introduced in 1977, with deliveries commencing in July of that year, the JetRanger III differs from the JetRanger II which it supplants in having an uprated engine, an enlarged and improved tail rotor mast and more minor changes. Some 3,000 commercial JetRangers had been delivered by the beginning of 1980, both commercial and military versions (including production by licensees) totalling more than 6,000. A light observation version of the JetRanger for the US Army is designated OH-58 Kiowa and a training version for the US Navy is known as the TH-57A SeaRanger. The JetRanger is built by Agusta in Italy as the AB 206, and at the beginning of 1980, Augusta was producing the JetRanger at a rate of six monthly and the parent company was producing 20 monthly.

230

BELL MODEL 206L-1 LONGRANGER II

Country of Origin: USA.

Type: Seven-seat light utility helicopter.

Power Plant: One 500 shp Allison 250-C28B turboshaft.

Performance: (At 3,900 lb/1 769 kg) Max. speed, 144 mph (232 km/h); cruise, 136 mph (229 km/h) at sea level; hovering ceiling (in ground effect), 8,200 ft (2 499 m), (out of ground effect), 2,000 ft (610 m); range, 390 mls (628 km) at sea level, 430 mls (692 km) at 5,000 ft (1 524 m).

Weights: Empty, 2,160 lb (980 kg); max. take-off, 4,050 lb (1 837 kg).

Dimensions: Rotor diam. 37 ft 0 in (11,28 m); fuselage length, 33 ft 3 in (10,13 m).

Notes: The Model 206L-1 Long Ranger II is a stretched and more powerful version of the Model 206B JetRanger III, with a long fuselage, increased fuel capacity, an uprated engine and a larger rotor. The Long Ranger is being manufactured in parallel with the JetRanger III and initial customer deliveries commenced in October 1975, prototype testing having been initiated on September 11, 1974. The Long Ranger is available with emergency flotation gear and with a 2,000-lb (907-kg) capacity cargo hook. In the aeromedical or rescue role the Long Ranger can accommodate two casualty stretches and two ambulatory casualties. The 206L-1 Long Ranger II was introduced in 1978, and production was 15 monthly at the beginning of 1980.

BELL MODEL 209 (AH-1S) HUEYCOBRA

Country of Origin: USA.
Type: Two-seat light attack helicopter.
Power Plant: One 1,800 shp Avco Lycoming T53-L-703 turboshaft.
Performance: Max. speed, 172 mph (277 km/h), (TOW configuration), 141 mph (227 km/h); max. climb, 1,620 ft/min (8,23 m/sec); hovering ceiling TOW configuration (in ground effect), 12,200 ft (3 720 m); max. range, 357 mls (574 km).
Weights: (TOW configuration) Empty, 6,479 lb (2 939 kg); max. take-off, 10,000 lb (4 535 kg).
Dimensions: Rotor diam, 44 ft 0 in (13,41 m); fuselage length, 44 ft 7 in (13,59 m).
Notes: A dedicated attack and anti-armour helicopter serving with the US Army (690 being converted from early AH-1G standard and 297 being built to AH-1S standards from outset), and being supplied to Israel, Morocco and Japan, the AH-1S can carry eight TOW missiles and is fitted with an M-197 20-mm cannon turret. The earlier AH-1G has been supplied to Israel and Spain, and twin-engined versions for the US Marine Corps are the AH-1J and AH-1T SeaCobra (see 1979 edition), the latter being an improved model with a 1,970 shp Pratt & Whitney T400-WV-402 coupled turboshaft. A total of 202 AH-1J SeaCobras (1,800 shp T400-CP-400) was supplied to Iran. The AH-1T utilises the dynamic components of the Model 214 helicopter.

BELL MODEL 214ST

Country of Origin: USA.

Type: Medium transport helicopter (19 seats).

Power Plant: Two 1,625 shp (limited to combined output of 2,250 shp) General Electric T700-T1C (CT7-2) turboshafts.

Performance: Max. cruising speed, 173 mph (278 km/h); econ. cruise, 155–167 mph (249–269 km/h); hovering ceiling (out of ground effect), 6,000 ft (1 830 m); range (with 20 min reserve), 460 mls (740 km).

Weights: Max. take-off, 16,500 lb (7 491 kg).

Dimensions: Rotor diam, 52 ft 0 in (15,85 m); fuselage length, 50 ft 1 in (15,26 m).

Notes: The Model 214ST is a significantly improved derivative of the Model 214B BigLifter (see 1978 edition), and both military and commercial models are planned. The Model 214ST test-bed was first flown in March 1977, and the first of three representative prototypes (one in military configuration and two for commercial certification) commenced its test programme during August 1979, production deliveries being scheduled to commence late 1981 or early 1982. As a high-density military transport, the Model 214ST will accommodate 17 troops and a tactical combat version will carry a crew of four and a 12-man squad, while the commercial model will accommodate 16 passengers. Development of the Model 214ST was originally initiated as an extrapolation of the Model 214A for the Iranian Army.

BELL MODEL 222

Country of Origin: USA.
Type: Eight/ten-seat light utility and transport helicopter.
Power Plant: Two 620 shp Avco Lycoming LTS 101-650C-2 turboshafts.
Performance: Max. cruising speed, 150 mph (241 km/h) at sea level, 146 mph (235 km/h) at 8,000 ft (2 400 m); max. climb, 1,730 ft/min (8,8 m/sec); hovering ceiling (in ground effect), 10,300 ft (3 135 m), (out of ground effect), 6,400 ft (1 940 m); range (no reserves), 450 mls (724 km) at 8,000 ft (2 400 m).
Weights: Empty equipped, 4,577 lb (2 076 kg); max. take-off (standard configuration), 7,650 lb (3 470 kg).
Dimensions: Rotor diam. 39 ft 9 in (12,12 m); fuselage length, 39 ft 9 in (12,12 m).
Notes: The first of five prototypes of the Model 222 was flown on August 13, 1976, an initial production series of 250 helicopters of this type being initiated in 1978, with production deliveries commencing in October 1979 and production rate building up to 14 monthly at the beginning of 1980, when some 150 had been ordered. Several versions of the Model 222 are on offer or under development, these including an executive version with a flight crew of two and five or six passengers and the so-called "offshore" model with accommodation for eight passengers and a flight crew of two. Options include interchangeable skids.

BELL MODEL 412

Country of Origin: USA.

Type: Fifteen-seat utility transport helicopter.

Power Plant: One 1,800 shp (1,308 shp take-off rating) Pratt & Whitney PT6T-3B turboshaft.

Performance: Max. speed, 149 mph (240 km/h) at sea level; cruise, 143 mph (230 km/h) at sea level, 146 mph (235 km/h) at 5,000 ft (1 525 m); hovering ceiling (in ground effect), 10,800 ft (3 290 m), (out of ground effect), 7,100 ft (2 165 m) at 10,500 lb/4 763 kg; max. range, 282 mls (454 km), (with auxiliary tanks), 518 mls (834 km).

Weights: Empty equipped, 6,070 lb (2 753 kg); max. take-off, 11,500 lb (5 216 kg).

Dimensions: Rotor diam, 46 ft 0 in (14,02 m); fuselage length, 41 ft 8½ in (12,70 m).

Notes: The Model 412, flown for the first time in August 1979, is an updated Model 212 Twin Two-Twelve (see 1979 edition) with a new-design four-bladed rotor, a shorter rotor mast assembly, and uprated engine and transmission systems, giving more than twice the life of the Model 212 units. Composite rotor blades are used and the rotor head incorporates elastomeric bearings and dampers to simplify moving parts. A second Model 412 prototype was scheduled to join the test programme late 1979, when more than 60 helicopters of this type had been ordered, with production deliveries to commence in 1981, anticipated production rate building up to 100 annually by 1983.

BOEING VERTOL CH-47D CHINOOK

Country of Origin: USA.

Type: Medium transport helicopter.

Power Plant: Two 4,500 shp Avco Lycoming T55-L-712 turboshafts.

Performance: Max. speed, 185 mph (298 km/h) at sea level; average cruise, 156 mph (251 km/h); max. climb, 2880 ft/min (14,63 m/sec); radius (with 14,322-lb/6 502-kg internal load), 115 mls (185 km), (with 15,775-lb/7 162-kg external load), 34 mls (56 km); mission radius, 115 mls (185 km).

Weights: Empty, 22,784 lb (10 344 kg); max. take-off 53,500 lb (24 290 kg).

Dimensions: rotor diam (each), 60 ft 0 in (18,29 m); fuselage length, 51 ft 0 in (15,55 m).

Notes: The CH-47D is the result of a modernisation programme of CH-47A, B and C Chinooks, and the first of three CH-47D Chinook prototypes (a conversion of a CH-47A) flew for the first time on May 11, 1979, with second and third prototypes (respectively conversions of a CH-47B and a CH-47C) following in June and August. The anticipated conversion programme calls for 148 CH-47As, 78 CH-47Bs and approximately 200 CH-47Cs to be brought up to CH-47D standards. The CH-47C is licence-built in Italy by Elicotteri Meridionali (a component of the Agusta group) which has supplied this helicopter to the Italian Army, and to Iran, Libya and Morocco. A commercial model will commence testing mid-1980.

HUGHES 500M-D TOW DEFENDER

Country of Origin: USA.

Type: Light anti-armour helicopter.

Power Plant: One 420 shp Allison 250-C20B turboshaft.

Performance: (At 3,000 lb/1 362 kg) Max. speed, 175 mph (282 km/h) at sea level; cruise, 160 mph (257 km/h) at 4,000 ft (1 220 m); max. inclined climb, 1,920 ft/min (9,75 m/sec); hovering ceiling (in ground effect), 8,800 ft (2 682 m), (out of ground effect), 7,100 ft (2 164 m); max. range, 263 mls (423 km).

Weights: Empty, 1,295 lb (588 kg); max. take-off (internal load), 3,000 lb (1 362 kg), (with external load), 3,620 lb (1 642 kg).

Dimensions: Rotor diam, 26 ft 5 in (8,05 m); fuselage length, 21 ft 5 in (6,52 m).

Notes: The Model 500M-D is a multi-role military helicopter derived, via the civil Model 500D, from the US Army's OH-6A Cayuse observation helicopter. The TOW Defender version is an anti-armour helicopter with 7,62-mm armour for the crew, engine compressor and fuel control, and provision for four TOW (Tube-launched Optically-tracked Wire-guided) missiles. Various alternative weapons may be fitted, including seven-round launchers for 2·75-in rockets, a 30-mm chain gun on the fuselage side or a 7,62-mm chain gun in an extendible ventral turret. The Defender is being manufactured in South Korea under a co-production arrangement.

HUGHES AH-64

Country of Origin: USA.

Type: Tandem two-seat attack helicopter.

Power Plant: Two 1,536 shp General Electric T700-GE-700 turboshafts.

Performance: Max. speed, 191 mph (307 km/h); cruise, 179 mph (288 km/h); max. inclined climb, 3,200 ft/min (16,27 m/sec); hovering ceiling (in ground effect), 14,600 ft (4 453 m), (outside ground effect), 11,800 ft (3 600 m); service ceiling, 8,000 ft (2 440 m); max. range, 424 mls (682 km).

Weights: Empty, 9,900 lb (4 490 kg); primary mission, 13,600 lb (6 169 kg); max. take-off, 17,400 lb (7 892 kg).

Dimensions: Rotor diam, 48 ft 0 in (14,63 m); fuselage length, 49 ft 4½ in (15,05 m).

Notes: Winning contender in the US Army's AAH (Advanced Attack Helicopter) contest, the YAH-64 flew for the first time on September 30, 1975. Two prototypes were used for the initial trials and the first of three more with fully integrated weapons systems commenced trials on October 31, 1979, planned total procurement comprising 536 AH-64s. The AH-64 is armed with a single-barrel 30-mm gun based on the chain-driven bolt system and suspended beneath the forward fuselage, and eight BGM-71A TOW anti-armour missiles may be carried, alternative armament including 16 Hellfire laser-seeking missiles. Target acquisition and designation and a pilot's night vision systems will be used.

KAMOV KA-25 (HORMONE A)

Country of Origin: USSR.

Type: Shipboard anti-submarine warfare helicopter.

Power Plant: Two 900 shp Glushenkov GTD-3 turboshafts.

Performance: (Estimated) Max. speed, 130 mph (209 km/h); normal cruise, 120 mph (193 km/h); max. range, 400 mls (644 km); service ceiling, 11,000 ft (3 353 m).

Weights: (Estimated) Empty, 10,500 lb (4 765 kg); max. take-off, 16,500 lb (7 484 kg).

Dimensions: Rotor diam (each), 51 ft $7\frac{1}{2}$ in (15,74 m); approx. fuselage length, 35 ft 6 in (10,82 m).

Notes: Possessing a basically similar airframe to that of the Ka-25K (see 1973 edition) and employing a similar self-contained assembly comprising rotors, transmission, engines and auxiliaries, the Ka-25 serves with the Soviet Navy primarily in the ASW role but is also employed in the utility and transport roles. The ASW Ka-25 serves aboard the helicopter cruisers *Moskva* and *Leningrad,* and the carriers *Kiev* and *Minsk,* as well as with shore-based units. A search radar installation is mounted in a nose radome, but other sensor housings and antennae differ widely from helicopter to helicopter. There is no evidence that externally-mounted weapons may be carried. Each landing wheel is surrounded by an inflatable pontoon surmounted by inflation bottles. The Hormone-A is intended for ASW operations whereas the Hormone-B is used for over-the-horizon missile targeting.

MBB BO 105L

Country of Origin: Federal Germany.

Type: Five/six-seat light utility helicopter.

Power Plant: Two 550 shp Allison 250-C28C turboshafts.

Performance: Max. speed, 168 mph (270 km/h) at sea level; max. cruise, 157 mph (252 km/h) at sea level; max. climb, 1,970 ft/min (10 m/sec); hovering ceiling (in ground effect), 13,1220 ft (4 000 m), (out of ground effect), 11,280 ft (3 440 m); range, 286 mls (460 km).

Weights: Empty, 2,756 lb (1 250 kg); max. take-off, 5,291 lb (2 400 kg), (with external load), 5,512 lb (2 500 kg).

Dimensions: Rotor diam, 32 ft 3½ in (9,84 m); fuselage length, 28 ft 1 in (8,56 m).

Notes: The BO 105L is a derivative of the BO 105CB (see 1979 edition) with uprated transmission and more powerful turboshaft for "hot-and-high" conditions. It is otherwise similar to the BO 105CB (420 shp Allison 250-C20B) which is continuing in production at the beginning of 1980, when more than 500 BO 105s (all versions) had been delivered and production was running at 10–12 monthly, and licence assembly was being undertaken in Indonesia and the Philippines. Deliveries to the Federal German Army of 227 BO 105M helicopters for liaison and observation tasks commenced late 1979, and 212 HOT-equipped BO 105s for the anti-armour role are being built simultaneously. The latter have uprated engines and transmission systems.

MBB-KAWASAKI BK 117

Countries of Origin: Federal German and Japan.
Type: Multi-purpose eight-to-twelve-seat helicopter.
Power Plant: Two 600 shp Avco Lycoming LTS 101-650B-1 turboshafts.
Performance: Max. speed, 171 mph (275 km/h) at sea level; cruise, 164 mph (264 km/h) at sea level; max. climb, 1,970 ft/min (10 m/sec); hovering ceiling (in ground effect), 13,450 ft (4 100 m), (out of ground effect), 10,340 ft (3 150 m); range (max. payload), 339 mls (545,4 km).
Weights: Empty, 3,351 lb (1 520 kg); max. take-off, 6,173 lb (2 800 kg).
Dimensions: Rotor diam, 36 ft 1 in (11,00 m); fuselage length, 32 ft 5 in (9,88 m).
Notes: The BK 117 is a co-operative development between Messerschmitt-Bölkow-Blohm and Kawasaki, the first of two flying prototypes commencing its flight test programme on June 13, 1979 (in Germany), with the second following on August 10 (in Japan), when manufacture of a pre-production batch of 10 BK 117s had begun, these being scheduled to fly from the second half of 1980, with production deliveries commencing mid-1981. MBB is responsible for the main and tail rotor systems, tail unit and hydraulic components, while Kawasaki is responsible for production of the fuselage, undercarriage, transmission and some other components. Several military versions are currently proposed.

MIL MI-14 (HAZE-A)

Country of Origin: USSR.
Type: Amphibious anti-submarine helicopter.
Power Plant: Two 1,500 shp Isotov TV-2 turboshafts.
Performance: (Estimated) Max. speed, 143 mph (230 km/h); max. cruise, 130 mph (210 km/h); hovering ceiling (in ground effect), 5,250 ft (1 600 m), (out of ground effect), 2,295 ft (700 m); tactical radius, 124 mls (200 km).
Weights: (Estimated) Max. take-off, 26,455 lb (12 000 kg).
Dimensions: Rotor diam, 69 ft 10¼ in (21,29 m); fuselage length, 59 ft 7 in (18,15 m).
Notes: The Mi-14 amphibious anti-submarine warfare helicopter, which serves with shore-based elements of the Soviet Naval Air Force, is a derivative of the Mi-8 (see 1978 Edition) with essentially similar power plant and dynamic components, and much of the structure is common between the two helicopters. New features include the boat-type hull, outriggers which, housing the retractable lateral twin-wheel undercarriage members, incorporate water rudders, a search radar installation beneath the nose and a sonar "bird" beneath the tailboom root. The Mi-14 may presumably be used for over-the-horizon missile targeting and for such tasks as search and rescue. It may also be assumed that the Mi-14 possesses a weapons bay for ASW torpedoes, nuclear depth charges and other stores. This amphibious helicopter reportedly entered service in 1975.

MIL MI-24 (HIND-D)

Country of Origin: USSR.
Type: Assault and anti-armour helicopter.
Power Plant: Two 1,500 shp Isotov TV-2 turboshafts.
Performance: (Estimated) Max. speed, 160 mph (257 km/h); max. cruise, 140 mph (225 km/h); hovering ceiling (in ground effect), 6,000 ft (1 830 m), (out of ground effect), 1,600 ft (790 m); normal range, 300 mls (480 km).
Weights: Normal take-off, 22,000 lb (10 000 kg).
Dimensions: Rotor diam, 55 ft 0 in (16,76 m); fuselage length, 55 ft 6 in (16,90 m).
Notes: The Hind-D version of the Mi-24 assault helicopter embodies a redesigned forward fuselage and is optimised for the gunship role and has tandem stations for the weapons operator (in the extreme nose) and pilot with individual canopies, the cockpit of the latter being raised to afford an unobstructed forward view. A four-barrel Gatling-type large-calibre machine gun is mounted in an offset chin turret, there are four wing pylons for rocket pods (32×55-mm) and endplate pylons at the wingtips carry rails for four Swatter antitank missiles. Apart from the Hind-D, the principal service versions of the Mi-24 are the Hind-A (see 1977 edition) armed assault helicopter featuring a flight deck for a crew of four, and the essentially similar Hind-C which has no nose gun and undernose sighting system, or missile rails at wingtips. The Hind-C and Hind-D are apparently complementary.

SIKORSKY S-61D (SEA KING)

Country of Origin: USA.

Type: Amphibious anti-submarine helicopter.

Power Plant: Two 1,500 shp General Electric T58-GE-10 turboshafts.

Performance: Max. speed, 172 mph (277 km/h) at sea level; inclined climb, 2,200 ft/min (11,2 m/sec); hovering ceiling (out of ground effect), 8,200 ft (2 500 m); range (with 10% reserves), 622 mls (1 000 km).

Weights: Empty equipped, 12,087 lb (5 481 kg); max. take-off, 20,500 lb (9 297 kg).

Dimensions: Rotor diam, 62 ft 0 in (18,90 m); fuselage length, 54 ft 9 in (16,69 m).

Notes: A more powerful derivative of the S-61B, the S-61D serves with the US Navy, as the SH-3D, 72 helicopters of this type following on production of 255 SH-3As (S-61Bs) for the ASW role for the US Navy, four being supplied to the Brazilian Navy and 22 to the Spanish Navy. Four similar aircraft have been supplied to the Argentine Navy as S-61D-4s and 11 have been supplied to the US Army/US Marine Corps Executive Flight Detachment as VH-3Ds. Licence manufacture of the S-61D is being undertaken in the United Kingdom (see page 252), in Japan for the Maritime Self-Defence Force and in Italy by Agusta for the Italian and Iranian and Peruvian (illustrated) navies. The SH-3G and SH-3H are upgraded conversions of the SH-3A.

SIKORSKY S-61R

Country of Origin: USA.
Type: Amphibious transport and rescue helicopter.
Power Plant: (CH-3E) Two 1,500 shp General Electric T58-GE-5 turboshafts.
Performance: (CH-3E at 21,247 lb/9 635 kg) Max. speed, 162 mph (261 km/h) at sea level; range cruise, 144 mph (232 km/h); max. inclined climb, 1,310 ft/min (6,6 m/sec); hovering ceiling (in ground effect), 4,100 ft (1 250 m); range with 10% reserves, 465 mls (748 km).
Weights: (CH-3E) Empty, 13,255 lb (6 010 kg); normal take-off, 21,247 lb (9 635 kg); max. take-off, 22,050 lb (10 000 kg).
Dimensions: Rotor diam, 62 ft 0 in (18,90 m); fuselage length, 57 ft 3 in (17,45 m).
Notes: Although based on the S-61A, the S-61R embodies numerous design changes, including a rear ramp and a tricycle-type undercarriage. Initial model for the USAF was the CH-3C with 1,300 shp T58-GE-1 turboshafts, but this was subsequently updated to CH-3E standards. The CH-3E can accommodate 25–30 troops or 5,000 lb (2 270 kg) of cargo, and may be fitted with a TAT-102 barbette on each sponson mounting a 7,62-mm Minigun. The HH-3E is a USAF rescue version with armour, self-sealing tanks, and refuelling probe, and the HH-3F Pelican is a US Coast Guard search and rescue model.

SIKORSKY CH-53E SUPER STALLION

Country of Origin: USA.
Type: Amphibious assault transport helicopter.
Power Plant: Three 4,380 shp General Electric T64-GE-415 turboshafts.
Performance: Max. speed, 196 mph (315 km/h) at sea level; max. cruise, 173 mph (278 km/h); hovering ceiling (in ground effect), 11,550 ft (3 525 m), (out of ground effect), 9,500 ft (2 900 m); max. range, 1,290 mls (2 075 km).
Weights: Operational empty, 33,000 lb (14 968 kg); max. take-off, 69,750 lb (31 638 kg).
Dimensions: Rotor diam., 79 ft 0 in (24,08 m); fuselage length, 73 ft 5 in (22,38 m).
Notes: The CH-53E is a growth version of the CH-53D Sea Stallion (see 1974 edition) embodying a third engine, an uprated transmission system, a seventh main rotor blade and increased rotor diameter. The first of two prototypes was flown on March 1, 1974, and the first of two pre-production prototypes flew on December 8, 1975, production orders authorising 20 by the beginning of 1980. The CH-53E can accommodate up to 56 troops in a high-density arrangement and can lift a 32,000-lb (14 515-kg) external load over a radius of 58 miles (93 km) at sea level in a 90 deg F temperature. The planned production programme envisages the acquisition from May 1980 of 49 helicopters of this type divided between the US Navy (16, and US Marine Corps (33).

SIKORSKY S-70 (UH-60A) BLACK HAWK

Country of Origin: USA.

Type: Tactical transport helicopter.

Power Plant: Two 1,543 shp General Election T700-GE-700 turboshafts.

Performance: Max. speed, 224 mph (360 km/h) at sea level; cruise, 166 mph (267 km/h); vertical climb rate, 450 ft/min (2,28 m/sec); hovering ceiling (in ground effect), 10,000 ft (3 048 m), (out of ground effect), 5,800 ft (1 758 m); endurance 2·3–3·0 hrs.

Weights: Design gross, 16,500 lb (7 485 kg); max. take-off, 22,000 lb (9 979 kg).

Dimensions: Rotor diam, 53 ft 8 in (16,23 m); fuselage length, 50 ft 0¾ in (15,26 m).

Notes: The Black Hawk was winner of the US Army's UTTAS (Utility Tactical Transport Aircraft System) contest, and contracts had been announced by beginning of 1980 for 200 examples. The first of three YUH-60As was flown on October 17, 1974, and a company-funded forth prototype flew on May 23, 1975. The Black Hawk is primarily a combat assault squad carrier, accommodating 11 fully-equipped troops, but it is capable of carrying an 8,000-lb (3 629-kg) slung load and can perform a variety of secondary missions, such as reconnaissance and troop resupply. The first production deliveries to the US Army were made in June 1979, with 36 delivered by the beginning of 1980.

SIKORSKY S-70L (SH-60B) SEAHAWK

Country of Origin: USA.

Type: Shipboard multi-role helicopter.

Power Plant: Two 1,630 shp General Electric T700-GE-400 turboshafts.

Performance: (Estimated) Max. cruise, 172 mph (277 km/h); max. vertical climb rate, 450 ft/min (2,28 m/sec); ceiling, 10,000 ft (3 050 m); time on station (at radius of 57 mls/92 km), 3 hrs, (at radius of 173 mls/278 km), 1 hr.

Weights: Mission loaded (ASW), 19,377 lb (8 789 kg), (anti-ship surveillance), 17,605 lb (7 985 kg).

Dimensions: Rotor diam, 53 ft 8 in (16,36 m); fuselage length, 50 ft 0¾ in (15,26 m).

Notes: The S-70L was selected by the US Navy on September 1, 1977, as winning contender in its LAMPS (Light Airborne Multi-purpose System) Mk. III helicopter, the first of five proto-types having been scheduled to fly in December 1979, and the US Navy having a requirement for 204 helicopters of this type with deliveries commencing at the end of 1983 under the designation SH-60B. The S-70L is a derivative of the UH-60A Black Hawk and is capable of carrying two homing torpedoes, 25 sonobuoys and an extensive range of avionics. It will serve aboard DD-963 destroyers, DDG-47 Aegis cruisers and FFG-7 guided-missile frigates as an integral extension of the sensor and weapons system of the launching vessel. The SH-60B has rotor blade and pylon folding.

SIKORSKY S-76 SPIRIT

County of Origin: USA.
Type: Fourteen-seat commercial transport helicopter.
Power Plant: Two 700 shp Allison 250-C30 turboshafts.
Performance: Max. speed, 179 mph (288 km/h); max. cruise, 167 mph (268 km/h); range cruise, 145 mph (233 km/h); hovering ceiling (in ground effect), 5,100 ft (1 524 m), (out of ground effect), 1,400 ft (427 m); range (full payload and 30 min reserve), 460 mls (740 km).
Weights: Empty, 4,942 lb (2 241 kg); max. take-off, 9,700 lb (4 399 kg).
Dimensions: Rotor diam, 44 ft 0 in (13,41 m); fuselage length, 44 ft 1 in (13,44 m).
Notes: The first of four prototypes of the S-76 flew on March 13, 1977, and customer deliveries commenced 1979, with 40 being delivered by the beginning of 1980, when a production rate of eight per month has been attained. The S-76 is unique among Sikorsky commercial helicopters in that conceptually it owes nothing to an existing military model, although it has been designed to conform with appropriate military specifications and military customers were included among contracts for some 280 helicopters of this type that had been ordered by the beginning of 1980, and 80–100 are scheduled for delivery during the year. The S-76 may be fitted with extended-range tanks, cargo hook and rescue hoist. The main rotor is a scaled-down version of that used by the UH-60.

WESTLAND WG 13 LYNX

Country of Origin: United Kingdom.
Type: Multi-purpose, ASW and transport helicopter.
Power Plant: Two 900 shp Rolls-Royce BS.360-07-26 Gem 100 turboshafts.
Performance: Max. speed, 207 mph (333 km/h); max. continuous sea level cruise, 170 mph (273 km/h); max. inclined climb, 1,174 ft/min (11,05 m/sec); hovering ceiling (out of ground effect), 12,000 ft (3 660 m); max. range (internal fuel), 391 mls (629 km); max. ferry range (auxiliary fuel), 787 mls (1 266 km).
Weights: (HAS Mk 2) Operational empty, 6,767–6,999 lb (3 069–3 174 kg); max. take-off, 9,500 lb (4 309 kg).
Dimensions: Rotor diam, 42 ft 0 in (12,80 m); fuselage length, 39 ft 1¼ in (11,92 m).
Notes: The first of 13 development Lynxes was flown on March 21, 1971, with the first production example (an HAS Mk 2) flying on February 10, 1976. By the beginning of 1979, production rate was nine per month and 285 were on order, including 26 for the French Navy, 60 for the Royal Navy, 100 for the British Army, eight for the Danish Navy, as for the German Navy, nine for the Brazilian Navy, six for Norway and 16 for the Netherlands Navy. The Lynx AH Mk 1 is the British Army's general utility version and the Lynx HAS Mk 2 is the ASW version for the Royal Navy. Licence manufacture is to be undertaken in Egypt.

WESTLAND WG 30

Country of Origin: United Kingdom.
Type: Transport and utility helicopter.
Power Plant: Two 1,060 shp Rolls-Royce Gem 41-1 turbo-shafts.
Performance: Max. speed (at 10,500 lb/4 763 kg), 163 mph (263 km/h) at 3,000 ft (915 m); hovering ceiling (in ground effect), 7,200 ft (2 195 m), (out of ground effect), 5,000 ft (1 525 m); range (seven passengers), 426 mls (686 km).
Weights: Operational empty (typical), 6,880 lb (3 120 kg); max. take-off, 11,750 lb (5 330 kg).
Dimensions: Rotor diam, 43 ft 8 in (13,31 m); fuselage length, 47 ft 0 in (14,33 m).
Notes: The WG 30, flown for the first time on April 10, 1979, is a private venture development of the Lynx (see opposite page) featuring an entirely new fuselage offering a substantial increase in capacity. Aimed primarily at the multi-role military helicopter field, the WG 30 has a crew of two and in the transport role can carry 17–22 passengers. Commitment to the WG 30 at the time of closing for press covers only the flight development of two prototypes aimed at certification during 1981, but a decision was expected early 1980 for the ordering of long-lead time items for an initial production batch for delivery before the end of 1981. The WG 30 utilizes more than 85 per cent of the proven systems of the WG 13 Lynx. Versions of the WG 30 for the civil market are forseen.

WESTLAND SEA KING

Country of Origin: United Kingdom (US licence).
Type: Anti-submarine warfare and search-and-rescue helicopter.
Power Plant: Two 1,060 shp Rolls-Royce Gem 41-1 turboshafts.
Performance: Max. speed, 143 mph (230 km/h); max. continuous cruise at sea level, 131 mph (211 km/h); hovering ceiling (in ground effect), 5,000 ft (1 525 m), (out of ground effect), 3,200 ft (975 m); range (standard fuel), 764 mls (1 230 km), (auxiliary fuel), 937 mls (1 507 km).
Weights: Empty equipped (ASW), 13,672 lb (6 201 kg), (SAR), 12,376 lb (5 613 kg); max. take-off, 21,000 lb (9 525 kg).
Dimensions: Rotor diam, 62 ft 0 in (18,90 m); fuselage length, 55 ft 9¾ in (17,01 m).
Notes: The Sea King Mk. 2 is an uprated version of the basic ASW and SAR derivative of the licence-built S-61D (see page 244), the first Mk. 2 being flown on June 30, 1974, and being one of 10 Sea King Mk. 50s ordered by the Australian Navy. Twenty-one have been ordered for the Royal Navy as Sea King HAS Mk. 2s, 15 examples of a SAR version for the RAF as Sea King HAR Mk. 3s, and 15 of a transport version for the Royal Navy as Sea King HC Mk. 4s (illustrated above). The last-mentioned version first flew on September 26, 1979. A total of 213 Westland-built derivatives of the S-61D had been ordered by the beginning of 1980.

ACKNOWLEDGEMENTS

The author wishes to record his thanks to the many aircraft manufacturers that have supplied information and photographs for inclusion in this volume and to the following sources of copyright photographs: Flug Revue International, pages 158 and 162; Howard Levy, pages 166, 222 and 248; Israir, page 112, and Stephen P. Peltz, page 114. The three-view silhouette drawings published in the volume are copyright Pilot Press Limited and may not be reproduced without prior permission.

INDEX OF AIRCRAFT TYPES

255

Printed and bound in Great Britain by
Butler & Tanner Ltd, Frome and London